THE
VULNERABLE
OBSERVER

THE

ANTHROPOLOGY THAT

VULNERABLE

BREAKS YOUR HEART

OBSERVER

RUTH BEHAR

BEACON PRESS | BOSTON

BEACON PRESS
Boston, Massachusetts
www.beacon.org

Beacon Press books
are published under the auspices of
the Unitarian Universalist Association of Congregations.

Printed in the United States of America

25 24 23 22   8 7 6 5 4 3 2 1

This book is printed on acid-free paper that meets the uncoated paper
ANSI/NISO specifications for permanence as revised in 1992.

Text design and composition by Kim Arney

The following essays are reprinted by permission of the publishers.
They have been edited and revised for this book.

"Death and Memory: From Santa María del Monte to Miami Beach,"
Cultural Anthropology 6, 3 (August 1991): 346–384.

"My Mexican Friend Marta Who Lives across the Border from Me in Detroit,"
in Bruce Grindal and Frank Salamone, eds., *Bridges to Humanity: Narratives on
Anthropology and Friendship* (Prospect Heights, Ill.: Waveland Press, 1995).

"The Girl in the Cast," in Marianne Gullestad, ed., *Imagined Childhoods*
(Oslo: Scandinavian University Press, 1996).

"Viajero" by Dulce María Loynaz is reprinted by permission of the author.
From *Versos, 1920–1938* in *Poesia Completa* (La Habana, Cuba:
Editorial Letras Cubanas, 1993).

Library of Congress Cataloging-In-Publication Data
Behar, Ruth
The vulnerable observer : anthropology that breaks your heart / Ruth Behar.
p. cm.
Includes bibliographical references and index.
ISBN 978-0-8070-0713-6 (paperback) | ISBN 978-0-8070-0780-8 (ebook)
1. Participant observation—Psychological aspects. 2. Anthropologists—
Attitudes. 3. Anthropologists—Psychology. I. Title.
GN346.4.B44 1996
301'.0723—dc20
96-11409

For

DEB CHASMAN
my vulnerable editor

Viajero

Yo soy como el viajero
que llega a un puerto y no lo espera nadie;
Soy el viajero tímido que pasa
entre abrazos ajenos y sonrisas
que no son para él . . .
Como el viajero solo
que se alza el cuello del abrigo
en el gran muelle frío . . .

Traveler

I am like the traveler
who reaches the port and no one awaits him;
I am the timid traveler who walks
among strangers embracing and smiles
not meant for him . . .
Like the lone traveler
who raises his overcoat collar
on the great, cold wharf . . .

—DULCE MARÍA LOYNAZ

CONTENTS

CHAPTER 1

THE VULNERABLE OBSERVER

It is customary to call books about human beings either toughminded or tenderminded. My own is neither and both, in that it strives for objectivity about that tendermindedness without which no realistic behavioral science is possible.

—GEORGE DEVEREUX, From Anxiety to Method

I n 1985 an avalanche in Colombia buried an entire village in mud. Isabel Allende, watching the tragedy on television, wanted to express the desperation she felt as she helplessly observed so many people being swallowed by the earth. In her short story "Of Clay We Are Created," Allende writes about Omaira Sánchez, a thirteen-year-old girl who became the focus of obsessive media attention. News-hungry photographers, journalists, and television camera people, who could do nothing to save the girl's life, descended upon her as she lay trapped in the mud, fixing their curious and useless eyes on her suffering. Amid that horrid audience of onlookers, which included Allende herself watching the cruel "show" on the screen, she places the photographer Rolf Carlé. He too has been looking, gazing, reporting, taking pictures. Then something snaps in him. He can no longer bear to watch silently from behind the camera. He will not document tragedy as an innocent bystander. Crouching down in the mud, Rolf Carlé throws aside his camera and flings his arms around Omaira Sánchez as her heart and lungs collapse.

The vulnerable observer par excellence, Rolf Carlé incarnates the central dilemma of all efforts at witnessing. In the midst of a massacre, in the face of torture, in the eye of a hurricane, in the aftermath of an earthquake, or even, say, when horror looms apparently more gently in memories that won't recede and so come pouring forth in the late-night quiet of a kitchen, as a storyteller opens her heart to a story listener, recounting hurts that cut deep and raw into the gullies of the self, do you, the observer, stay behind the lens of the camera, switch on the tape recorder, keep pen in hand? Are there limits—of respect, piety, pathos—that should not be crossed, even to leave a record? But if you can't stop the horror, shouldn't you at least document it?

Allende assumed that once her story was published, Omaira would disappear from her life. But in *Paula*, her moving memoir of her daughter's sudden and rapid death from porphyria, she finds herself returning to Omaira's story, which has acquired the eerie power of fiction that foretells the future. This time, Allende is painfully close to tragedy, no television screen acting as buffer. Like Rolf Carlé, she must get "down in the mud" with her daughter, who has fallen into a coma, her gaze "focused beyond the horizon where death begins." Sitting at the bedside of Paula, a Sleeping Beauty who will never awaken, Allende, with pen in hand, gives up the possibility of imagining other worlds through fiction. Surrendering to the intractableness of reality, she feels herself setting forth on "an irreversible voyage through a long tunnel; I can't see an exit but I know there must be one. I can't go back, only continue to go forward, step by step, to the end."[1]

For me, anthropology is about embarking on just such a voyage through a long tunnel. Always, as an anthropologist, you go elsewhere, but the voyage is never simply about making a trip to a Spanish village of thick-walled adobe houses in the Cantabrian Mountains, or a garden apartment in Detroit where the planes circle despondently overhead, or a port city of cracking pink columns and impossible hopes known as La Habana, where they tell me I was born. Loss, mourning, the longing for memory, the desire to enter into the world around you and having no idea how to do it, the fear of observing too coldly or too distractedly or too raggedly, the rage of cowardice, the insight that is always arriving late, as defiant hindsight, a sense of the utter uselessness of writing anything and yet the burning desire to write something, are the stopping places along the way. At the end of the voyage, if you are lucky, you catch a glimpse of a lighthouse, and you are grateful. Life, after all, is bountiful.

But surely this is not the anthropology being taught in our colleges and universities? It doesn't sound like the stuff of which Ph.D.'s are made. And definitely it isn't the anthropology that will win you a grant from the National Science Foundation. Nor, to be perfectly honest, is it the anthropology I usually tell people I do. People, say, like my Aunt Rebeca, who is asking me—over a midnight snack of Cuban bread and *café con leche* in bustling Puerto Sagua, where people are devouring, as if there were no tomorrow, enormous plates of steak with browned onions and glistening plantains—why I went into anthropology.

No sé decirte cómo fué . . . I was very young. . . . I wanted to write. . . . A teacher had faith in me. . . . They gave me a fellowship to study anthropology. . . . I went to live in a Spanish village. . . . There I learned how to recite a rosary and heard my Sephardic ancestors whispering in my ears, "Shame, shame. . . ." Over the years this anthropology became a way to always be taking leave, a way to always be returning, a way to always be packing and unpacking suitcases, as if I were mimicking the history of our own family, traveling from Europe to the other America, to this America, this Puerto Sagua, not the one of the same name left behind on the island, but this one here where the Cuban bread and café con leche never run dry. . . ."

And then before I have answered her first question, my Aunt Rebeca asks, "Rutie, *pero dime*, what is anthropology?" While I hesitate, she confidently exclaims, "The study of people? And their customs, right?"

Right. People and their customs. Exactly. *Así de fácil.* Can't refute that. Somehow, out of that legacy, born of the European colonial impulse to know others in order to lambast them, better manage them, or exalt them, anthropologists have made a vast intellectual cornucopia. At the anthropological table, to which another leaf is always being added, there is room for studies of Greek death laments, the fate of socialist ideals in Hungary and Nicaragua, Haitian voodoo in Brooklyn, the market for Balinese art, the abortion debate among women in West Fargo, North Dakota, the reading groups of Mayan intellectuals, the proverbs of a Hindi guru, the Bedouin sense of honor, the jokes Native Americans tell about the white man, the plight of Chicana cannery workers, the utopia of Walt Disney World, and even, I hope, the story of my family's car accident on the Belt Parkway shortly after our arrival in the United States from Cuba (the subject to which, in fact, we turned that night in Puerto Sagua, my Aunt Rebeca telling me they heard about it when they opened up the Sunday *Times* the next morning and, in shock, read the news).

Anthropology, to give my Aunt Rebeca a grandiose reply, is the most fascinating, bizarre, disturbing, and necessary form of witnessing left to us at the end of the twentieth century. As a mode of knowing that depends on the particular relationship formed by a particular anthropologist with a particular set of people in a particular time and place, anthropology has always been vexed about the question of vulnerability. Clifford Geertz says, "You don't exactly penetrate another culture, as the masculinist image would have it. You put yourself in its way and it bodies forth and enmeshes you."[2] Yes, indeed. But just how far do you let that other culture enmesh you? Our intellectual mission is deeply paradoxical: get the "native point of view," *pero por favor* without actually "going native." Our methodology, defined by the oxymoron "participant observation," is split at the root: act as a participant, but don't forget to keep your eyes open. Lie down in the mud in Colombia. Put your arms around Omaira Sánchez. But when the grant money runs out, or the summer vacation is over, please stand up, dust yourself off, go to your desk, and write down what you saw and heard. Relate it to something you've read by Marx, Weber, Gramsci, or Geertz and you're on your way to doing anthropology.

Nothing is stranger than this business of humans observing other humans in order to write about them. James Agee, sent by *Fortune* magazine on a mission to bring back an enticing story about dirt-poor farmers in the American South during the Depression, furiously wished he could tear up a clump of earth with a hoe and put that on the page and publish it. Instead, he wrote *Let Us Now Praise Famous Men*, a troubled meditation about his fear of exploiting the lives of southern tenant farmers, which forms part of the very account in which he was trying, with an exaggerated sense of propriety and shame, to describe the contours of those same lives.

In different ways, writers like Agee and Allende arrive at that tenderminded toughmindedness which George Devereux suggested thirty years ago should be the goal of any inquiry involving humans observing other humans. Devereux, an ethnopsychiatrist, believed that observers in the social sciences had not yet learned how to make the most of their own emotional involvement with their material. *What happens within the observer* must be made known, Devereux insisted, if the nature of what has been observed is to be understood. The subjectivity of the observer, he noted, "influences the course of the observed event as radically as 'inspection' influences ('disturbs') the behavior of an electron." The observer "*never* observes the behavioral event which 'would have taken place' in his absence, nor hears an account identical with that which the same narrator would give to another person." Yet because there is no clear and easy route by which to confront the self who observes, most professional observers develop defenses, namely, "methods," that "reduce anxiety and enable us to function efficiently." Even saying, "I am an anthropologist; this is fieldwork," is a classic form of the use of a method to drain anxiety from situations in which we feel complicitous with structures of power, or helpless to release another from suffering, or at a loss as to whether to act or observe.

Although he acknowledged the subjective nature of all social knowledge, for Devereux self-reflexivity was not an end in itself. Recognizing subjectivity in social observation was a means to a more important end—achieving significant forms of objectivity and therefore truly "true" science.[3] Regardless of whether or not we aspire to science (and I, at least, do not), accepting Devereux's premise about the relentless subjectivity of all social observation still leaves us with a practical problem—How do you write subjectivity into ethnography in such a way that you can continue to call what you are doing ethnography? Should we be worried that a smoke alarm will blare in our ears when the ethnography grows perilously hot and "too personal"?

In *Works and Lives*, Clifford Geertz comes at this question by suggesting that ethnographies are a strange cross between author-saturated and author-evacuated texts, neither romance nor lab report, but something in between. Unlike Devereux, remaking anthropology into a better science is not Geertz's primary concern. Instead, Geertz considers the later phases of the ethnographic process, the moment of writing and the reception of the anthropologist's text. How is it, Geertz wants to know, that anthropologists (a handful of them, anyway) transfigure their observations of other people and places into such persuasive rhetoric that afterward those people and places are unimaginable except through the texts of their authors? As Geertz asserts, "One can go look at Azande again, but if the complex theory of passion, knowledge, and causation that Evans-Pritchard said he discovered there isn't found, we are more likely to doubt our own powers than we are to doubt his—or perhaps simply to conclude that the Zande are no longer themselves."

An anthropologist's conversations and interactions in the field can never again be exactly reproduced. They are unique, irrecoverable, gone before they happen, always in the past, even when written up in the present tense. The ethnography serves as the only proof of the anthropologist's voyage, and the success of the enterprise hinges on how gracefully the anthropologist shoulders what Geertz calls the "burden of authorship." The writing must convey the impression of "close-in contact with far-out lives."

Who decides if this goal has been achieved? Ultimately, says Geertz, the grounds for accepting one anthropologist's truth over another are extremely "person-specific" (not "personal," he insists, leaving the distinction obscure). For example, Oscar Lewis forcefully disputed the veracity of Robert Redfield's vision of life in Tepotzlán in his own restudy of the same Mexican town, but this did not make the Redfieldian text obsolete. On the contrary, by shifting attention to a diametrically opposed vision of the same people and place, Lewis only succeeded in proving that he and Redfield were *both* right, that they were "different sorts of minds taking hold of different parts of the elephant."[4]

Aware as he is that in anthropology everything depends on the emotional and intellectual baggage the anthropologist takes on the voyage, Geertz, like Devereux, still seems to me to embrace the cause of subjectivity with only half a heart. Devereux champions vulnerability for the sake of science. Geertz, in turn, repeatedly shows us that anthropology—as practiced by greats such as Lévi-Strauss, Evans-Pritchard, Malinowski, and Benedict—is resolutely person-specific and yet somehow not "personal." Ironically, he reserves his harshest criticism for ethnographic writing that takes an autobiographical stance on the pursuit we call "fieldwork," this always going elsewhere, the voyage through the long tunnel. Geertz insists it is inappropriate to interiorize too much "what is in fact an intensely public activity."

But just how public an activity is the work of the anthropologist? Yes, we go and talk to people. Some of these people even have the patience and kindness and generosity to talk to us. We try to listen well. We write fieldnotes about all the things we've misunderstood, all the things that later will seem so trivial, so much the bare surface of life. And then it is time to pack our suitcases and return home. And so begins our work, our hardest work—to bring the ethnographic moment back, to resurrect it, to communicate the distance, which too quickly starts to feel like an abyss, between what we saw and heard and our inability, finally, to do justice to it in our representations. Our fieldnotes become palimpsests, useless unless plumbed for forgotten revelatory moments, unexpressed longings, and the wounds of regret. And so, even though we start by going public, we continue our labor through introspection. And then we go public again, and if the first time we dealt in something that came dangerously close to tragedy, the second time around we are definitely in the theater of farce as our uncertainty and dependency on our subjects in the field is shifted into a position of authority back home when we stand at the podium, reading our ethnographic writing aloud to other stressed-out ethnographers at academic conferences held in Hiltons where the chandeliers dangle by a thread and the air-conditioning chills us to the bone. Even Geertz recognizes there is a problem: "We lack the language to articulate what takes place when we are in fact at work. There seems to be a genre missing."[5]

Consider this book a quest for that genre.

F ortunately, I am not alone in this quest.
   What does it mean, for example, that an established professor of psychiatry at Johns Hopkins University School of Medicine, who co-authored a standard medical text on manic-depressive illness, should now choose to reveal, in a memoir, that she is herself a wounded healer, for she suffers from manic-depressive illness? In *An Unquiet Mind*, a memoir of moods and madness, Kay Redfield Jamison refuses to conceal her transformation of anxiety into method. She announces at the start of her book that she isn't sure what the consequences will be of giving public voice to her illness: "I have had many concerns

about writing a book that so explicitly describes my own attacks of mania, depression, and psychosis, as well as my problems acknowledging the need for ongoing medication. Clinicians have been, for obvious reasons of licensing and hospital privileges, reluctant to make their psychiatric problems known to others. These concerns are often well warranted. I have no idea what the long-term effects of discussing such issues so openly will be on my personal and professional life but, whatever the consequences, they are bound to be better than continuing to be silent. I am tired of hiding, tired of misspent and knotted energies, tired of the hypocrisy, and tired of acting as though I have something to hide."[6]

Later in the book, Jamison tells of her encounter with Mogens Schou, a Danish psychiatrist, who is responsible for the introduction of lithium as a treatment for manic-depressive illness. On a boat ride down the Mississippi River in New Orleans he asks her point-blank, "Why are you *really* studying mood disorders?" She hesitates to answer and he goes on to tell her why he has studied mood disorders—because of depression and manic-depressive illness in his family. "It had been this strong personal motivation that had driven virtually all of his research," and it is Mogens who encourages her, in turn, to use her own experiences in her research, writing, and teaching. Nevertheless, she continues to feel anxious: "Will my work now be seen by my colleagues as somehow biased because of my illness? . . . If, for example, I am attending a scientific meeting and ask a question, or challenge a speaker, will my question be treated as though it is coming from someone who has studied and treated mood disorders for many years, or will it instead be seen as a highly subjective, idiosyncratic view of someone who has a personal ax to grind? It is an awful prospect, giving up one's cloak of academic objectivity. But, of course, my work *has* been tremendously colored by my emotions and my experiences. They have deeply affected my teaching, my advocacy work, my clinical practice, and what I have chosen to study: manic-depressive illness."[7]

Not only is Jamison a wounded healer; she lives with the knowledge that, if her illness were to get out of control, she would cease to be able to heal at all. With devastating honesty, she admits she has no guarantee she will remain healthy on a steady dose of lithium and therapy. As she remarks, "I know that I listen to lectures about new treatments for manic-depressive illness with far more than just a professional interest. I also know that when I am doing Grand rounds at other hospitals, I often visit their psychiatric wards, look at their seclusion rooms and ECT suites, wander their hospital grounds, and do my own internal ratings of where I would choose to go if I had to be hospitalized. There is always a part of my mind that is preparing for the worst, and another part of my mind that believes if I prepare enough for it, the worst won't happen."[8]

One of my colleagues, a medical anthropologist, tells me that the main reason Jamison is able to make herself so vulnerable at this moment in time is because of advances in the field of biochemistry, which have led to new understandings of the biochemical roots of depression, making it possible to control the illness through medical supervision and drugs. Science, in other words, has drained the shame out of depression. We saw that process at work when Colin Powell, at the press conference where he announced he wouldn't run for president, answered in quite measured tones, when the subject of his wife's depression was raised, that yes, indeed, she suffers from depression, but she is receiving medical treatment, just like he takes pills that control his blood pressure, "most of the time."

Yet if science makes it possible for the unspeakable to be spoken, if science opens borders previously closed, why is Jamison so anxious about her revelations? Why is she not more comforted by science? Like other scholars stretching the limits of objectivity, she realizes there are risks in exposing oneself in an academy that continues to feel ambivalent about observers who forsake the mantle of omniscience.

Increasingly, scholars are willing to take such risks. Among the interdisciplinary works emerging from this turn toward vulnerable observation, there is literary critic Alice Kaplan's *French Lessons*, which takes on her own fascination with the French language in the context of Jewish critical thinking about fascism, and the uneasy complicity of French writers who collaborated with the Nazis during World War II. In *Landscape for a Good Woman*, historian Carolyn Kay Steedman offers an account of her mother's life that reveals the inability of British working-class history to account for her mother's resentful and unfulfilled desires for the things of the world. In *Dancing with the Devil*, anthropologist José Limón locates himself as a Chicano not only within his fieldwork but within the long history of military, folkloric, and anthropological representations of Mexicans in the United States, which precede his arrival in the field.[9]

No one objects to autobiography, as such, as a genre in its own right. What bothers critics is the insertion of personal stories into what we have been taught to think of as the analysis of impersonal social facts. Throughout most of the twentieth century, in scholarly fields ranging from literary criticism to anthropology to law, the reigning paradigms have traditionally called for distance, objectivity, and abstraction. The worst sin was to be "too personal." But if you're an African-American legal scholar writing about the history of contract law and you discover, as Patricia Williams recounts in *The Alchemy of Race and Rights*, the deed of sale of your own great-great-grandmother to a white lawyer, that bitter knowledge certainly gives "the facts" another twist of urgency and poignancy. It undercuts the notion of a contract as an abstract, impersonal legal document, challenging us to think about the universality of the law and the pursuit of justice for all.[10]

Of course, as is the case with any intellectual trend, some experiments work out better than others. It is far from easy to think up interesting ways to locate oneself in one's own text. Writing vulnerably takes as much skill, nuance, and willingness to follow through on all the ramifications of a complicated idea as does writing invulnerably and distantly. I would say it takes yet greater skill. The worst that can happen in an invulnerable text is that it will be boring. But when an author has made herself or himself vulnerable, the stakes are higher: a boring self-revelation, one that fails to move the reader, is more than embarrassing; it is humiliating. To assert that one is a "white middle-class woman" or a "black gay man" or a "working-class Latina" within one's study of Shakespeare or Santería is only interesting if one is able to draw deeper connections between one's personal experience and the subject under study. That doesn't require a full-length autobiography, but it does require a keen understanding of what aspects of the self are the most important filters through which one perceives the world and, more particularly, the topic being studied. Efforts at self-revelation flop not because the personal voice has been used, but because it has been poorly used, leaving unscrutinized the connection, intellectual and emotional, between the observer and the observed.

Vulnerability doesn't mean that anything personal goes. The exposure of the self who is also a spectator has to take us somewhere we couldn't otherwise get to. It has to be essential to the argument, not a decorative flourish, not exposure for its own sake. It has to move us beyond that eclipse into inertia, exemplified by Rolf Carlé, in which we find ourselves identifying so intensely with those whom we are observing that all possibility of reporting is arrested, made inconceivable. It has to persuade us of the wisdom of not leaving the writing pad blank.

The charge that all the variants of vulnerable writing that have blossomed in the last two decades are self-serving and superficial, full of unnecessary guilt or excessive bravado, stems from an unwillingness to even consider the possibility that a personal voice, if creatively used, can lead the reader, not into miniature bubbles of navel-gazing, but into the enormous sea of serious social issues. Rather than facing the daunting task of assessing the newly vulnerable forms of writing emerging in the academy, critics like Daphne Patai choose to dismiss them all as evidence of a "nouveau solipsism."[11]

For Patai, my chapter on "the biography in the shadow" in *Translated Woman* is a case in point.[12] There I related my experience of getting tenure at Michigan within a study that explored the life story of Esperanza, a Mexican street peddler. I did so not to treat our struggles as equivalent but rather to show how different I am from Esperanza, because I had attained the privilege (indeed, not without a struggle) that allowed me to bring Esperanza's story across the border. I also reflected on how my Latina background affected my university's decision to grant me tenure. Officials first classified me as Latina because of my Cuban roots, then withdrew the identification because of my Jewish roots, and finally designated me a Latina again when they granted me tenure to boost their statistics on affirmative action hirings. This experience called into question my ability to depict Esperanza's mixed identity, on the one hand of Indian descent, on the other cut off from much of her Indian heritage by centuries of colonialism. Was my portrait of her as reductionist, shifting, even hurtful as the university's characterization of me?[13]

It is precisely this chapter, which upsets the academic critics, that has brought so many readers to my ethnography and made them want to listen to a Mexican peddler's life story. I have received several letters from women and men who say that relating my own story made the book whole for them. A woman of Welsh/German ancestry writes, "It's 10:30 at night and I'm crying. I've just finished your book *Translated Woman*, flipping between the last chapter and the footnotes, between my WASP life and my daughter's and yours and Esperanza's; I feel such gratitude for your (that's plural) courage and empathy in the arduous journey toward understanding that I'm writing my first ever fan letter at the age of 57." A Chicana anthropology student in Los Angeles told me the book empowered her doubly: she could see her mother in Esperanza and she could see herself in me. Another woman, of mixed Colombian and Puerto Rican background, told me in a letter: "I was so glad to hear you're exploring the dilemmas regarding positions of power and negotiation of entry that I too struggle with in doing ethnography. *Translated Woman* has brought both *you* and Esperanza to voice. You are both helping me come to voice, as well." A man in New York, who remembered we had been fellow students in college, wrote: "I was touched by the honesty and courage that I felt it took for you, an academic, to write a book as personal as this one."

What impresses me about these responses (besides, of course, the tremendous kindness of people who take the time to write such encouraging letters) is that readers need to see a connection between Esperanza and me, despite our obvious differences, and they need to see a connection back to themselves as well. In responding to my response to Esperanza, readers always also tell me something of their own life stories and their own struggles. Since I have put myself in the ethnographic picture, readers feel they have come to know me. They have poured their own feelings into their construction of me and in that way come to identify with me, or at least their fictional image of who I am. These responses have taught me that when readers take the voyage through anthropology's tunnel it is themselves they must be able to see in the observer who is serving as their guide.

When you write vulnerably, others respond vulnerably. A different set of problems and predicaments arise which would never surface in response to more detached writing. What is the writer's responsibility to those who are moved by her writing? Devereux spoke in great detail of the observer's countertransference, but what about the reader's? Should I feel good that my writing makes a reader break out crying? Does an emotional response lessen or enhance intellectual understanding? Emotion has only recently gotten a foot inside the academy and we still don't know whether we want to give it a seminar room, a lecture hall, or just a closet we can air out now and then.

Even I, a practitioner of vulnerable writing, am sometimes at a loss to say how much emotion is bearable within academic settings. Last fall, at a feminist anthropology conference at the University of Michigan organized by the graduate students, I found myself in just such a dilemma as a new colleague prefaced her remarks by turning warmly toward me to say my work had given her permission to speak in ways that are taboo in the academy. Naturally I was flattered, but also I felt apprehensive. What would I find myself responsible for? She began to read, first from her ethnographic writing about spirit possession in India, giving detailed and thoughtful descriptions in a cool and controlled voice. Suddenly, she switched gears. Her tone grew passionate as she recounted her own experience of being brutally beaten by a former husband in a possession trance. She had not read this section of her work aloud before and her voice trembled. Soon the tears came to her eyes. She had to stop several times to catch her breath. By the end, she was sobbing.

The room was packed. All the available seats were taken and there were people standing in the back. In an effort to create a more feminist and egalitarian environment, the students had arranged the chairs in a circle, so there was a huge gaping hole, a cavern, in the middle of the room. When my colleague had finished speaking, a terrible silence, like a dark storm cloud, descended upon everyone. A part of me wished the cavern in the middle of the room would open up and swallow us all, so we wouldn't have to speak.

After what seemed an eternity, another anthropology colleague, in her kindest voice, tried to take charge of the situation by commenting on the disparity between the two voices—the detached ethnographic voice and the exceedingly emotional personal voice. After a while, I too spoke, feeling obliged to speak. I took up where my colleague left off, and wondered aloud how we, as ethnographers, might go about writing emotion into the personal material without draining it all from the ethnography. My colleague, I realized, had made an all-too-common mistake, which I had come to recognize in my own writing: she paced her story in such a way that the ethnography moved along, steady, like a train cutting through a field, and then, *Boom! Bang! Crash!* There was the wrenching personal story of the suffering anthropologist. How, I asked—of my colleague and of myself—might we make the ethnography as passionate as our autobiographical stories? What would that take? And how might we unsettle expectations by writing about ourselves with more detachment and about others with all the fire of feeling? Can we give both the observer and the observed a chance at tragedy? As I spoke, people in the audience nodded their heads. Everyone seemed relieved that I, the champion of personal writing, was putting autobiography back in its place as the handmaiden of ethnography.

My new colleague had by this time calmed down and wiped away her tears. Even though I had responded sensibly and given her what everyone took to be a very constructive comment, I felt like I had failed her. What kept me glued to my chair, unable to rise and embrace her? Like Omaira Sánchez, she'd been in trouble. Unlike Rolf Carlé, I had watched her from a distance, sinking into the cavern in the middle of the room.

The image of my colleague, alone before the cavern, flashed before my eyes again when I was in Cuba early this year attending a women's conference about writing and art. A young writer, reading her fiction aloud for the first time, grew so nervous that her body shook convulsively. She tried to read, but she couldn't keep her hands still long enough to hold up her notebook. Immediately, one after another, the older, established writers present leaped to her side and put their arms around her. Soon, she was reading, still shaking but concentrating on her story. In fact, she went way over her time. After being politely asked to cut her reading short, she had become a furious prima donna. I felt she had lost her right to any sympathy. Later in the conference, another woman, talking about divided Cuban families, began to cry and could no longer go on speaking. This time the audience spontaneously began to applaud, louder and louder, as if to finish her sentence. Many of those clapping were crying, too.

In Michigan, all that emotion scared us, scared me. So we stayed quiet, like obedient schoolchildren waiting for the teacher to scold us. And, sadly, I became that teacher, ruler in hand, making my own knuckles bleed.

To write vulnerably is to open a Pandora's box. Who can say what will come flying out? When I began, nine years ago, to make my emotions part of my ethnography, I had no idea where this work would take me or whether it would be accepted within anthropology and the academy. I began with a sense of urgency, a desire to embed a diary of my life within the accounts of the lives of others that I was being required to produce as an anthropologist. As a student I was taught to maintain the same strict boundary Malinowski had kept between his ethnography and his autobiography. But I'd reached a point where these forms of knowing were no longer so easily separated. And I came to realize that in much contemporary writing, these genres seemed to have exchanged places, ethnography becoming more autobiographical while autobiography had become more ethnographic.[14] As I wrote, the ethnographer in me wanted to know: Who is this woman who is writing about others, making others vulnerable? What does she want from others? What do the others want from her? The feminist in me wanted to know: What kind of fulfillment does she get—or not get—from the power she has? The novelist in me wanted to know: What, as she blithely goes about the privilege of doing research, is the story she isn't willing to tell?

Unconsciously at first, but later with more direction, I chose the essay as a genre through which to *attempt* (the original meaning of *essai*, or essay) the dialectic between connection and otherness that is at the center of all forms of historical and cultural representation.[15] The essay has been described as "an act of personal witness. The essay is at once the inscription of a self and description of an object." An amorphous, open-ended, even rebellious genre that desegregates the boundaries between self and other, the essay has been the genre of choice for radical feminists and cultural critics pursuing thick description.[16] And perhaps too, through the essay, anthropologists can come closest to fulfilling those illicit desires, so frequently alluded to in Malinowski's diary, of longing to write poetry, fiction, drama, memoir, anything but ethnography, that second-fiddle genre we have inherited.[17]

The more colleagues called upon me to present my work at conferences, workshops, and public lectures, the more desperate I felt; time was being taken away from me to do the *really creative* writing I wanted to do. That *really creative* writing was being perpetually put on hold, perpetually postponed. So I began to write public performance pieces which were fringed with snatches of that other writing. These pieces—which I presented like a truant schoolgirl, hesitantly, apologetically, as failures to produce what I was expected to produce—called for an intellectual *and* emotional engagement from the listener.

Gradually I realized why I was acting like a truant schoolgirl: my anthropological mask was peeling off. Committed to speaking as a Latina, to speaking, therefore, from the margins rather than from the center of the academy, I was coming to see that I had been playing the role of the second-rate *gringa*. I felt uneasy with the entitlement I had earned, of being able to speak from the "macro" position, of being able to speak unequivocally and uncritically for others. At the same time, I began to understand that I had been drawn to anthropology because I had grown up within three cultures—Jewish (both Ashkenazi and Sephardic), Cuban, and American—and I needed to better connect my own profound sense of displacement with the professional rituals of displacement that are at the heart of anthropology. As these ideas grew clearer in my mind, I found myself resisting the "I" of the ethnographer as a privileged eye, a voyeuristic eye, an all-powerful eye. Every ethnography, I knew, depended on some form of ethnographic authority. But as an ethnographer for whom the professional ritual of displacement continually evoked the grief of diaspora, I distrusted my own authority. I saw it as being constantly in question, constantly on the point of breaking down.

What first propelled me to try to write ethnography in a vulnerable way was the intense regret and self-loathing I felt when my maternal grandfather died of cancer in Miami Beach while I was away doing a summer's fieldwork in Spain. The irony was heightened by the fact that I had gone to Spain, knowing that my grandfather was dying, with a mission to gather material for an academic paper I'd been asked to write for a panel on "the anthropology of death." To talk about death with the aging peasant villagers who had initiated me into anthropology became at once a distressing exercise in surrealism and the most charged moment of empathy for the suffering of others that I have ever experienced. Hesitantly, I put down my first impressions in an early version of "Death and Memory" and presented it at the annual meeting of the American Anthropological Association. The audience was moved, but I emerged shaken and uncertain. What had I done? By turning some of the spotlight on myself had I drawn attention away from "bigger" issues in the study of the anthropology of death? What was I seeking from my colleagues? Empathy? Pity? Louder applause?

I was so confused I put the essay away and returned to writing about women's witchcraft in eighteenth-century Mexico. Two summers later, in 1989, I pulled out the essay again. By then my status had shifted dramatically. I had won a major award that confirmed for my parents that they were right to leave Cuba. Michigan, in turn, granted me tenure, the immigrant dream of security. "Be grateful to this country," my mother said. "In Cuba you would have been cutting sugarcane." The daughter, at last, was reaping the rewards of her parents' displacement. It was a moment when I ought to have been happy, but I'd fallen into a state of mourning. I was mourning a loss for which I knew I deserved no sympathy—the loss of my innocence when I let Michigan toy with my most intimate sense of identity and buy me out. I didn't say a word about any of this in "Death and Memory." The essay drew its emotional force from the unspeakableness of my sorrow.[18]

Other essays, mixing the personal and the ethnographic, quickly followed. From Spain, I went to Mexico, where the whole course of my life and work changed as I felt in my own flesh how the border between the United States and Mexico is, in Gloria Anzaldúa's words, "*una herida abierta* where the Third World grates against the first and bleeds."[19] *Translated Woman* is about a terrible irony: that Esperanza crosses the border as a literary wetback through my account of her life story. Yet, as I wrote *Translated Woman*, my friend Marta, also from Mexquitic, was settling down on this side of the border. In fact, she'd moved to Detroit, a half hour away from my home in Ann Arbor, and become my "neighbor." The border, the unforgiving border of race and class, I discovered, doesn't begin in Laredo. Marta's parents back in Mexquitic, who had shared their heart and house with us, had asked me to keep an eye on Marta, to try to save her from the dangers they knew all too well existed on the other side. I wrote "My Mexican Friend Marta Who Lives Across the Border from Me in Detroit" out of anguish, because I feared I'd not lived up to my part of the friendship, because I'd not done enough to stop Marta from punishing herself, forcing herself to become modern, by having a hysterectomy at twenty-six.[20]

Bill T. Jones has written that "all dance exists in memory." As he so lyrically put it, "The dancer steps, he pushes the earth away and is in the air. One foot comes down, followed by the other. It's over. We agree, dancer and watcher, to hold on to the illusion that someone flew for a moment." There is no physical evidence, says Jones. The material world is a place "that exists only in the moment, a place of illusion."[21] And the body itself, as I show in "The Girl in the Cast," is a site of memory, a place of illusion that is crushingly real. "The Girl in the Cast," the most personal essay in this book, is a confrontation with the most bitter fate that can befall an anthropologist. It is about the anthropologist who can go nowhere, the anthropologist who has turned agoraphobic and is unable to move beyond her bed, the anthropologist who has lost her way in the long tunnel and, this time, is sure she will never find the exit.

The tunnel I grew lost in was the tunnel leading back to Cuba. I took a long detour, via Spain and Mexico, to get back to this place where my childhood got left behind. And now I despair that for me Cuba will become just another anthropological fieldsite. But it may well have to be that or nothing. The dilemma of going home, the place that anthropologists are always leaving from rather than going to, is the subject of "Going to Cuba." Nowhere am I more vulnerable than in Cuba and among Cubans as I search for a way to become a bridge between the island and the diaspora. As a "promoter" of cultural bridges, I have an almost diabolical power—I can obtain visas for island friends to visit the United States, some of whom will choose to defect, some of whom will return to the envy and spite of those who have not had the chance to see the world beyond the ocean. And I ask myself: Back home, in Cuba, have I, the returning immigrant child whose parents spared her from having to cut sugarcane, become the ugliest of border guards?

This anthropology isn't for the softhearted.

N or is it for those who "marvel that anyone could choose a profession of such profound alienation and repeated loss."[22] But that is not the worst of it. No, the worst of it is that not only is the observer vulnerable, but so too, yet more profoundly, are those whom we observe.

An example of such vulnerability can be seen in the Italian movie rendition of "The Postman," which stunningly evokes the deep impression that the poet Pablo Neruda made upon "an ordinary man" in a small fishing village. The scene when this postman, his family, and neighbors pore over a foreign newspaper account of Neruda's sojourn in their village, expecting to find some mention of themselves, struck me as especially poignant in depicting the sense of loss and alienation experienced by those who took the poet-exile into their lives expecting that he, too, would take them into his own life with the same fullness of feeling. We anthropologists—merely poor relatives of Pablo Neruda—leave behind our own trail of longings, desires, and unfulfilled expectations in those upon whom we descend. About that vulnerability we are still barely able to speak.

S keptics might reasonably ask: At a moment when the autobiographical voice is so highly commodified—most visibly in the talk shows of Oprah and Geraldo Rivera—shouldn't scholars write against the grain of this personalizing of culture rather than reproduce it? Indeed, a recent trend among some anthropologists is to work as overseers of large teams of assistants on big research projects, with themes ranging from multigenerational perspectives on women's perceptions of their bodies to the role played by race and class in achieving academic success among high school students of different ethnic groups. The tendency is to depersonalize one's connection to the field, to treat ethnographic work (only a small part of which is done personally by the principal investigator) as that which is "other" to the "self," and to accumulate masses of data that can be compared, contrasted, charted, and serve as a basis for policy recommendations, or at least as a critique of existing practices. This is not the only depersonalizing trend. A number of anthropologists accord prestige value to "high theory" and produce accounts that are starkly unpeopled about concepts like neocolonialism, transnationalism, and postmodernism, among other "isms." Still others, as I once did, have retreated to history, to the quiet of the archives and the study of the past, where presumably an observer can do less damage, not have to be quite so disturbingly present.

Clearly, vulnerability isn't for everyone. Nor should it be. Anthropology is wide-ranging enough to include many different ways of witnessing. But it seems to me that some of these depersonalizing trends reflect a fear that the personal turn in the academy has gone too far and must be stopped before all hell breaks loose. But hell, I fear, has already broken loose: autobiography has emerged, for better or worse, as the key form of storytelling in our time, with everyone doing it, from Shirley MacLaine to Colin Powell to professors of French and psychiatry. Isn't it a pity that scholars, out of some sense of false superiority, should try to rise above it all?

In anthropology, which historically exists to "give voice" to others, there is no greater taboo than self-revelation. The impetus of our discipline, with its roots in Western fantasies about barbaric others, has been to focus primarily on "cultural" rather than "individual" realities. The irony is that anthropology has always been rooted in an "I"—understood as having a complex psychology and history—observing a "we" that, until recently, was viewed as plural, ahistorical, and nonindividuated.

Lately, anthropologists have been pushing at that irony, seeking another voice in anthropology that can accommodate complex I's and we's both here and there. This has led to a retheorization of genres like the life history and the life story, and the creation of hybrid genres like self-ethnography and ethnobiography. Personal narratives have a long tradition in anthropology, stemming from the studies of Native American cultures conducted by the first generation of anthropologists in the United States. The assumption behind the early quest for personal narratives was that native cultures had been broken, like ceramic pots, and the best you could do was study them in bits and pieces, from key individuals, who in telling their stories brought to light the disappearing, and often disappeared, lifeways of a group.[23]

The genres of life history and life story are merging with the *testimonio*, which speaks to the role of witnessing in our time as a key form of approaching and transforming reality. Producing testimony became a crucial therapeutic tool in the treatment of people who suffered psychological trauma under state terrorism. It was practiced in Europe with Holocaust survivors, and in Latin America it was introduced in the 1970s as a way of helping people come to terms with the psychic and social effects of political repression on their lives. Its use spread to Central America and it became a key genre for the expression of consciousness-raising among indigenous women leaders. *I, Rigoberta Menchú* became the symbol of that movement, in which the purpose of bearing witness is to motivate listeners to participate in the struggle against injustice.[24]

Another influence, in the United States, is the work of minority writers, like those included in the anthology *This Bridge Called My Back*, edited by the Chicana writers Gloria Anzaldúa and Cherríe Moraga, which discussed experiences of racism and discrimination as well as of coming to ethnic consciousness. These first-person narratives, written by those who previously had been more likely to be the ethnographized rather than the ethnographer, challenged monolithic views of identity in the United States, asserted the multiplicity of American cultures, and deconstructed various orientalisms, challenging the assumption that the anthropologist was the sole purveyor of ethnographic truth. In turn, the renewed interest in the tradition of African-American autobiography, with its origins in the personal narratives of ex-slaves, spoke to the importance of telling the stories of the "black self" as a form of protest against racist images that too eagerly collectivized the individual nuances and diverse life trajectories within the African-American experience.[25]

The last decade of meditation on the meaning of "native anthropology"—in which scholars claim a personal connection to the places in which they work—has opened up an important debate on what it means to be an insider in a culture. As those who used to be "the natives" have become scholars in their own right, often studying their home communities and nations, the lines between participant and observer, friend and stranger, aboriginal and alien are no longer so easily drawn. We now have a notable group of "minority" anthropologists with a range of ambivalent connections to the abandoned and reclaimed "homelands" in which they work. The importance of this "native anthropology" has helped to bring about a fundamental shift—the shift toward viewing identification, rather than difference, as the key defining image of anthropological theory and practice. We no longer, as Clifford Geertz put it in a much-quoted phrase, strain to read the culture of others "over the shoulders of those to whom they properly belong." We now stand on the same plane with our subjects; indeed, they will only tolerate us if we are willing to confront them face to face.[26]

These shifts, in tandem with the feminist movement's assertion that the "personal is political," have changed the way scholars in a wide range of disciplines think about the subject and subjectivity of their work. Feminist writers within the academy have devoted a considerable amount of energy to reflecting on biography and autobiography, and the difficult question of how women are to make other women the subjects of their gaze without objectifying them and thus ultimately betraying them.[27] The rethinking of objectivity being carried out by feminists who study the sciences—among them Evelyn Fox Keller, Sandra Harding, Donna Haraway, and Hillary Rose—has likewise put at the top of the agenda Devereux's dream of doing social science more subjectively so it will be more objective. As Sandra Harding puts it, "The beliefs and behaviors of the researcher are part of the empirical evidence for (or against) the claims advanced in the results of research. *This* evidence too must be open to critical scrutiny no less than what is traditionally defined as relevant evidence."[28] Or, in the words of Donna Haraway, "Location is about vulnerability; location resists the politics of closure, finality."[29] At the end of the road for feminist science is a vision of utopia—where objectivity will be so completely revised that situated knowledges will be tough enough to resist the coups of dictatorial forms of thought.

Literary criticism has likewise been moving toward a more vulnerable and situated view of the critic's task. A famous early example is Jane Tompkins's "Me and My Shadow," a piece of literary criticism that is continually "disrupted" by reflections about the author's bodily presence as she writes—her stocking feet, looking out the window, deciding whether or not to go to the bathroom.[30] More recently, Susan Rubin Suleiman has reflected on these shifts: "When I was in graduate school at Harvard in the early sixties, it was understood that good academic writing—in my case, literary criticism—aimed for impersonality and objectivity. What did a poem or a novel or an essay mean? Or, if you were more sophisticated: How did a work mean, how was it 'put together' to produce a certain effect? These were the questions we were taught to ask, and the first rule we learned was that in answering them, one must never say 'I.' Nor, of course, should one make humorous remarks, or play on words, or try for 'literary' or 'poetic' effects, or in any other way seek to put one's self, noticeably, into one's critical writing." Today, Suleiman claims, those rules no longer exist. "It is now all right to say 'I' in writing about literature. . . . The line between 'literature' and 'writing about literature' has itself begun to waver. . . . Some critics are now read as poets and novelists are read: not only for what they have to say, but for their personal voice and style." Her essays, Suleiman says, are not "straight autobiography," but "mediated autobiography," where the exploration of the writer's self takes place indirectly, through the mediation of writing about another, in her case, the work of writers and artists of the twentieth century.[31]

Such mediation is at the center of the new feminist biographical criticism. Toril Moi, for example, undertakes a thorough reading of Simone de Beauvoir's literary corpus to show how Beauvoir, far from being a perfect feminist role model, struggled to incarnate freedom. In Beauvoir's fiction, Moi notes, there is "always a woman who sacrifices her independence for love"; in her autobiographies, on the other hand, "the ideal of the autonomous woman is always present."[32] Beauvoir's relationship with Sartre is examined closely and thoughtfully, and as Moi points out, Sartre's pact of freedom (basically, he traded two years of monogamy for a lifetime of infidelity) was paralleled by Beauvoir's myth of unity, the myth of the Sartre-Beauvoir couple.

That this myth often fell apart for Beauvoir was dramatized in the anxiety attacks witnessed by friends and acquaintances, in which she would burst into floods of tears in a café, and then just as suddenly she'd dry her tears, powder her face, straighten her clothes, and rejoin the conversation as if nothing had happened.[33] Yet Beauvoir refused Sartre's proposal of marriage and tried to overcome her "weakness" through strict schedules of walking and writing. She rejected the traditional bourgeois position of the married woman, but emotionally Beauvoir was bound to Sartre. Moi suggests that Beauvoir's depression, rooted in the fear of loss of love, caught up with her as she grew older, though she refused to pay it any attention.

According to Moi, "On every page of her letters to Sartre she complains about her loneliness and emotional neediness *and* assures him that she is perfectly happy, totally satisfied with his love for her, and that she cannot wish for a better life. But this precisely is what Freud understands by disavowal. . . . Beauvoir both sees and does not see her own sorrow." Moi speculates that Beauvoir seemed "under a compulsion to repeat her cycles of depression, anxiety and fear of abandonment throughout her life. . . . Perhaps the presence of pain, in the end, felt more comforting to her than the fearsome emptiness of existential freedom?" Moi concludes that "Beauvoir poignantly conveys to us what it cost her to become a woman admired by a whole world for her independence."[34]

Moi's feminist study of Beauvoir, like Kay Redfield Jamison's *An Unquiet Mind*, is part of a torrent of new writing about women and depression. These writings range from popular psychological texts (Maggie Scarf's *Unfinished Business*) to academic psychological studies (Dana Crowley Jack's *Silencing the Self*) to memoirs about depression (*Washington Post* reporter Tracy Thompson's *The Beast: A Reckoning with Depression*) to popular biographies (Diane Wood Middlebrook's *Anne Sexton*). In this literature there is a powerful implicit—and often also explicit—criticism of the North American male ethos of always keeping a stiff upper lip and pulling yourself up by your bootstraps. The women who write these accounts, whether about themselves or other women, point to weaknesses, are all too aware of dependencies, admit to the need for medication (lithium, Prozac), and allow themselves to be painfully honest—in ways that our great feminist heroine Simone de Beauvoir didn't dare—about how they deal with the emotional fallout of being intellectual women in the late twentieth century.

Vulnerability, in short, is here to stay. Critics can keep dismissing these trends as forms of "solipsism," but a lot of us are going to continue wearing our hearts on our sleeves. To what should we attribute these trends? Is it mere whining? Or have we entered, as they say in Cuba, *a special period?*

The brilliant and terrible shorthand, *el periodo especial*, began to be used in Cuba at the dawn of the 1990s, after the fall of the Berlin Wall and the collapse of the Soviet Union. The cold war, it appeared, was over. The communist world was gone, toppled by free markets and capitalism. For Cuba, a defiant socialist island within spitting distance of the great capitalist mecca, which had depended on the socialist bloc for economic and ideological support, this was the beginning of the end. A wild scramble for food, fuel, and dollars ensued, and the key symbols of prerevolutionary decadence—tourism, prostitution, and foreign capitalist investment—returned with a vengeance. As doctors and dentists fixed up their cars and became cab drivers, and former revolutionaries swallowed their pride and dug up the addresses of their relatives in Miami to ask for a couple of dollars to buy cooking oil, the old revolutionary social values of reciprocity and laboring for the common good grew confused. What had the years of sacrifice—always for the sake of a messianic time not yet arrived—finally yielded? How had an island of utopian dreamers become so desperately vulnerable?

Cuba's *special period* epitomizes a more widespread loss of faith in master texts, master ideologies, steadfast truths, and monolithic ways of imagining the relation between self and community. In different ways, the rest of the world is also living through a special period. So many intellectual, political, socioeconomic, and emotional transformations are unfolding simultaneously as our century comes to a close. From the global arena to the intimate stirrings of the human heart, the disintegration of the old world order has provoked, as the writer Margaret Randall suggests, "a general reevaluation of stories we once accepted at face value, whatever our position in the fray."[35] New stories are rushing to be told in languages we've never used before, stories that tell truths we once hid, truths we didn't dare acknowledge, truths that shamed us.

As with the island of Cuba, everything has already happened and everything has yet to happen. And that is absolutely terrifying, but maybe, finally, it will prove absolutely liberating.

People and their customs. . . . I can hear my Aunt Rebeca asking: "Do you learn anything about Spaniards, Mexicans, Jews, Cubans, Jubans from reading these essays?" And I imagine myself replying, "Only insofar as you are willing to view them from the perspective of an anthropologist who has come to know others by knowing herself and who has come to know herself by knowing others. You should know that my one major vulnerability, my Achilles' heel, which I always thought was a problem in my becoming an anthropologist, is that I can't read a map. I'm the sort of person who gets lost just going around the corner. I think I got through school because they stopped teaching geography in American universities."

If you don't mind going places without a map, follow me.

CHAPTER 2

DEATH AND MEMORY

From Santa María del Monte to Miami Beach

*In memory of Maximo Glinsky (1902–1987), Justa Llamazares
Ferreras (1904–1989), Isaac Behar (1905–1989)*

*Like those birds that lay their eggs only in other species' nests,
memory produces in a place that does not belong to it.*

—MICHEL DE CERTEAU, The Practice of Everyday Life

*Flaccid, diseased cells are swarming and swelling inside my bones
and I have little time left. Of course I've waited too long before
writing this and now it is late, probably too late. Like beginning
to write at twilight with no lamp as the darkness falls. And there
is no light now. There was some a little while ago and I should
have written then. I also had some within me, a deep blue light
the colour of Iris which now and then I could see far inside my
body and which glowed and gave me great comfort. But it is really
dark now, my blue light has deserted me and it is getting very late.*

—ALLON WHITE, "Too Close to the Bone: Fragments of
an Autobiography" in *London Review of Books* (1989)

I had been a regular visitor to Santa María del Monte, a
northern Spanish village whose permanent inhabitants are
mainly elderly farmers, since the summer of 1978 when, at
twenty-one, I went as an anthropology graduate student to
get my first taste of fieldwork, and of rural life. I was accompanied by my young husband-to-be, who made the journey

with me to Spain without my parents' knowledge. With David I formed a unit, and we were tagged *la pareja* ("the couple"). Walking hand-in-hand along village dirt roads, we projected an image not so much of romance as of innocence; many people, in the first days, asked if we were brother and sister. I had been raised in New York City and had only the vaguest ideas about farming. I had gone on to learn what I could of Spanish peasant history and culture, producing a dissertation about a topic that life had not prepared me for, and embarking, a little hesitantly, on an academic career. In the summer of 1987, after a three-year absence, I was returning again with the book in hand that I had written, in English, about the history of the village, hoping, almost childishly, for the approval of village people. I was returning, as well, with my eleven-month-old son, answering at last people's incessant queries during years of visits as to when we would have children. I felt a great need to return, to show people my book and my child. I had been away for a while, and I wanted to explore new subjects with my longtime interlocutors—in particular, their ideas about Catholicism and priests, and, more uncertainly, their attitudes toward their own impending deaths. Letters from Santa María announcing one death and then another made it clear that these interlocutors, the elderly farmers of the village, were not going to last many years longer. I had to get back to see them.

But in that summer of 1987 my grandfather, or Zayde, as we called him in Yiddish, was dying of cancer in Miami Beach. He was one family member I adored unequivocally, with infatuation. Why I adored him so much I couldn't begin to explain. A bond had been formed between us in a childhood I had no memory of, a childhood spent in Havana. Zayde, my mother told me, would pass by our apartment building every day on his way to open his lace store. Under our window he would clap his hands just once and I would go rushing out to meet him. I loved him with a child's immense and selfless love, but I had also grown to love him with the adult woman's appreciation of his independence and vulnerability. We spoke little since Zayde did not like to talk (being suspicious of those who talked too much), and we always spoke in Spanish.

He was dying and I wanted to call and ask if he wanted me by him. I had gone to see him in May shortly after his cancer had been diagnosed. When I entered the apartment he was asleep in the reclining chair in the *cuartito*, the little room with the big television. He was already very thin. But when he woke up and we talked I could see that he was not going to accept death. Why was the doctor refusing to see him, he wanted to know. Why did all food smell and taste horrible? Yet Zayde cheered up so much during our visit that he almost didn't seem ill anymore. He took a bite of an omelette I made. He sat with us at the table. He held my child, his first great-grandchild, on his lap. When we said good-bye at the door he said to me, *"La primer nieta, eso es algo grande"* ("The first grandchild [which I had been], that's a great thing"). I came back not believing that he was dying.

I struggled that summer with the desire to stay in Miami Beach, to watch over him and help him to die. I had never helped anyone to die before and I had only the crudest idea of what it might mean to act toward an end that I myself deeply feared. One thing I knew: that to help Zayde to die I had to acknowledge that he was dying. Yet even if I could come to terms with his impending death, could he, could my mother, could the rest of the family? I spoke to my mother about wanting to stay and not go to Spain until Zayde's end. This led her to speak of her own guilt and preoccupations. Should she quit her secretarial job in New York to go to Miami Beach herself and be with him? She had already taken off all the time she could, and she was working overtime mornings and afternoons to save up days to be with him later on, when she would be most needed. My aunt told my mother that she thought it wrong to put aside one's plans and sit as if waiting for him to die. Life had to go on. My grandfather, I also knew, had never wanted to appear weak or pitiful before the family; if one patted him on the back too adoringly, he would double over and pretend to be a bent-over old man hobbling with a cane. He always stood very straight and had a brisk step. Not wanting to displace my mother, and hoping my grandfather would wait for me, I decided to go to Spain. I went, I think, with a fleeting, unspoken hope of witnessing another, less repressive, way of dying; but, more consciously, I went with the sanctioned importance of continuing my work, for life, after all, had to go on.

We arrived the evening before Corpus Christi and the following day at mass we were greeted by everyone in turn, the women greeting me first in the church portal, the men greeting David outside. When I stepped out of the church, Leonardo Mirantes, a man I deeply admired for his sharp historical memory, approached me quietly and, instead of a greeting, announced in an almost imperceptible voice, "This April I lost Ramona." The tears flowed down his cheeks. A sharp and articulate man of great intellectual zest, with a fine memory for dates and prices of goods in the past, Leonardo, now eighty-one, had received the last sacraments years before after a heart attack, and had surprised everyone by continuing to live, energetically as ever, outwearing three pacemakers. But, with the loss of his wife of fifty-three years, his spirit seemed broken. While the experience of death was especially fresh for Leonardo, he was not the only one to spontaneously speak of it; with everyone I spoke to, we would recite the litany of the dead, recalling one by one all the people I had known who had died in the last few years. Angel Mirantes, another village elder and cousin of Leonardo, speaking to me of the recent changes and improvements in village life, which had come too late for people of his generation to fully enjoy, said in his loud, clear shepherd's voice, "For us, there is only the tomb."

I t is obvious to my friends in Santa María that it is not just as individual elderly people that they are approaching death, but as a declining rural social class of peasant smallholders who can remember planting the wheat that went into their bread. Spain today is no longer the rural society that it was fifty years ago.[1] Then the Franco regime glorified rural life and the image of rural traditionalism, claiming, as in an article published in 1937 in a Leonese daily, that "Spanish life has to be disinfected with the healthy airs that blow in the fertile valleys of our mountains and in the ample horizons of our plains. . . . Tomorrow's peasant Spain will be the source of our greatness and of our virtues."[2] Blaming the city for "infecting" the nation with the vices of modernism, Francoist ideology inverted "the common image of the country [as] an image of the past and the common image of the city [as] an image of the future."[3] Postwar hunger and the scarcity in an isolated Spain drew people to migrant work in Northern Europe. And the Franco regime, in a later technocratic phase, would put forth a program of rapid industrialization aided by foreign investment (largely from the United States in exchange for four naval bases), tourism, and the remittances of emigrants gone to work in Northern Europe.[4] As the rural exodus took form in the 1960s and 1970s, the regime, once an enemy of city life and city proletariats, actively supported the industrial expansion that ushered Spain, rather abruptly, into the world of late capitalism.

Eventually, the young left the villages not to work in industry, but, encouraged by their own peasant parents, simply to leave the village, which had become symbolic of every sort of dead end. Thus the peasants who had been the object of so much romanticism were transformed into a marginal people, whose values and culture offered little worthy of emulation to a modern, urban Spain. Meanwhile, that modern, urban Spain, in a final act of resistance against the previous social asceticism, took refuge in rampant consumerism.[5] The villages were deserted, left to become one big cemetery for those old folk who had stayed behind. Writing in 1961 of a deserted village in Burgos, Miguel Delibes spoke of how "its winding streets, invaded by weeds and nettles, without a dog's bark or a child's laugh to break the silence, enclose a pathetic gravity, the lugubrious air of the cemetery."[6] Yet people recognized the sad necessity of the rural exodus at a time of population and capitalist expansion. The villages acquired perhaps an eerie stillness, but they also became places that afforded an unprecedented increase in the standard of living for those who did stay behind to work their resources less competitively.

While high unemployment plagues an otherwise booming, rapidly industrializing Spain, there is intense prosperity consciousness, and village people themselves speak of how much better off they are than they were in the past. They have televisions, radios, bathrooms, stainless steel sinks, things they did not have ten, twenty years ago; they go on excursions with church groups to other parts of Spain and even to France and Portugal.

Yet these villagers, who not too long ago worked (and, in some cases, continue to work) their fields with sickles, scythes, and teams of oxen, have come to feel socially excluded and useless. Sixto Mirantes, a longtime friend and participant in my work who is just about to turn seventy, wrote me a letter in June of 1988 in which he takes a mental trip around the village and stops at virtually every doorstep, pointing to yet another closed house. "The house closed," becomes his refrain as he lists the litany of deaths and departures.

"Well, about Santa María, what can I tell you? That every time there are fewer of us. I think that before the year two thousand it will have disappeared. Most of the houses are closed up. Felicidad died. He [her husband] went with his children. The house closed. At Baudilio's, only Sidor [an unmarried son] is there. You know, Vitaliano and Barista can no longer manage. They left to join their sons. The house closed. Luis we buried a month ago. Onorina [his wife] went with her daughter. The house closed. As for our neighbor, Balbino, it [their house] is open only on Sundays and during vacations. The rest of the time they reside in León. The upper barrio, as you know, [is occupied] on weekends and during vacations, otherwise there are hardly any people. Well, let's see if you return soon so we can see the young man [my son]. We want very much to see him and talk with you again. I am superfluous in everything [*Yo estoy de más para todo*]."

In the autobiography written shortly before his death, Luis Buñuel, the filmmaker, described the horror he felt at his mother's loss of memory at the end of her life, which made her forget who her children were and even who she was. The horror of this loss of memory, Buñuel says, is that it "can erase an entire life . . . without memory we are nothing."[7] A similar statement is made with respect to social, rather than individual, memory by Shmuel Goldman, a key speaker in Barbara Myerhoff's *Number Our Days*. As an aging Jew he spoke of the terror and pathos he felt at growing old because the little town in Poland he had grown up in was gone, "erased like a line of writing. . . . No way back remains because nothing is there, no continuation. Then life itself, what is its worth to us? Why have we bothered to live? All this is at an end. For myself, growing old would be altogether a different thing if that little town was there still. All is ended."[8]

There is a similar horror, I think, about the death that looms over small villages like Santa María, with their 100 or so inhabitants, taking away one elderly peasant villager after another. With each death, a part of that lived memory that connected every villager to a peasant past is erased, made unrecoverable. Sixto Mirantes's letter poignantly reveals that Santa María as a community is, in a profound sense, dying; at least the Santa María he and others of his generation knew is dying. Whether the community will physically vanish, as he seems to imply, or whether a different use and meaning will be given to the community that will, thereby, recreate it, remains to be seen. Certainly, there are signs of revitalization.[9] But Sixto, like other elderly villagers, feels left out, feels he has arrived too late.

Death has acquired a harsh significance for him and other village elderly, who are acutely aware that the reproduction of their society and culture has been truncated, brought to a standstill. Yet they await their deaths convinced that they are leaving behind a world that is much better than the world they knew, and many times better than the one their parents and grandparents knew. So much confidence have they lost in the rural religious culture within which they grew up that they actually seem glad that the reproduction of their culture has come to an end. They are plagued, not by nostalgia, but by a sense of having lived anachronistically for too long. "Every image of the past," wrote Walter Benjamin, "that is not recognized by the present as one of its own concerns threatens to disappear irretrievably."[10] The collective readiness for death that I sense among the elderly peasants of Santa María is, sadly, I think, a readiness to die without being reborn in historical memory, to die once and for all. Death, now more than ever before, is the death of memory.

The sense of discontinuity that is so heightened in old peasant communities like Santa María with their aging populations is, however, none other than the more general condition of modern memory, which, if we follow Pierre Nora, is always already history. What Nora has called "the acceleration of history—an increasingly rapid slippage of the present into a historical past that is gone for good, a general perception that anything and everything may disappear"—is, he suggests, the mark of our age.[11] Fear and anxiety about this continual slippage of the present into the past has made the archive the receptacle of remembering in our time, and history the place for the reconstitution of memory out of the dutifully collected "remains, documents, images, speeches, any visible signs of what has been, as if this burgeoning dossier were to be called upon to furnish some proof to who knows what tribunal of history."[12] Nora highlights three forms of modern memory: archive-memory (just seen), distance-memory (because the past is "given to us as radically other . . . a world apart"), and duty-memory, the sense of responsibility that weighs upon the individual, as if an inner voice is saying, "It is I who must remember"; as if one's "salvation ultimately depends on the repayment of an impossible debt."[13] There is no question that this essay is ultimately about duty-memory.

Those words of Sixto's, "I am superfluous in everything," resonate in my mind now as I rewrite this essay yet one more time, just as the words of Angel Mirantes, "For us, there is only the tomb," kept resonating for me during the summer of 1987. My thoughts that summer were mired in death. I couldn't forget that my grandfather was dying; that everything I was living an ocean away in the space of a village in Spain was being lived in the time frame of his dying. Anthropology is constantly about displacements; that summer I displaced my fears about my grandfather's death onto my interlocutors in Santa María, asking them the questions that I couldn't ask my own family in order to work through the anticipation of my own grief. It is the taped transcripts of those conversations, in which I am not the most cogent participant, rather than observations of death behavior, that form the crux of this essay.

We lived that summer, for the first time, in the village house of an upper-middle-class family. Polonia, the mother, an articulate widow in her late sixties, had married a military man and left the village for Madrid in the 1940s, where she had raised her two daughters and son; her daughters married professional men, an architect and an engineer, and her son became a respected doctor in an oncology ward in Madrid. Polonia was perhaps the first person to use the village as a vacation site; she would return every summer with her two daughters and her son, so they would get to know their peasant grandparents and learn to wipe mud and dung from their shoes. Polonia still returns to Santa María every summer with her daughter Rufi, in her early forties, and Rufi's husband and two teenage sons. Their house in the village has been studiously left in the old style; it is the only house in which the kitchen faces the courtyard rather than the street and in which the furnishings are all antique. Rufi had generously invited us to spend the month at their house and to do so as their guests. As an educated middle-class woman, and an outsider to rural life like me, Rufi had a sense of the ethnographic mission and often played the role of ethnographer better than I did during our many conversations about the past. We talked one afternoon about the death of Polonia's mother.

Polonia began: "When it was my mother, we [she and her sister] shrouded her. And Justa. She died at night, at four, at three or so in the morning. We shrouded her between the three of us, my sister, Justa, and I. Florencio [her brother-in-law] was here too, my husband was also here, which was curious, it was the fiesta—"

Rufi interrupted her to ask a generalizing question: "But how did you wash them?"

Her mother shrugged. "You wash them."

"With a towel, a sponge?"

"Yes, you wash them very well. No, nothing, it doesn't mean anything, because it is a normal body."

Rufi, playing the ethnographer, offers an explanation. "Why do you wash them, so that they will be clean when they get to heaven?" Rufi's zeal to interpret and draw conclusions—perhaps because it offers too close a mirror of me in ethnographic costume—makes me cringe in my seat.

"I don't know. These are customs."

Rufi turns to me and says: "It's folkloric, isn't it, Ruth?"

I, trying my best, intercept with a snatch of information I have picked up from an old will. "Yes, customs. Sometimes they dress them up in nun's or monk's clothes."

And Polonia: "Yes, sometimes they used to put tunics on them."

Rufi adds: "Here I think they put on their best Sunday clothes, right?"

"Yes, their best clothes, yes that's what one puts on them."

"It must be to present themselves before God, clean," says Rufi.

While Polonia speaks with casual ease of washing her mother's corpse, her daughter, speaking for the ethnographer and horrified at the thought of having to come into such close contact with a dead body, can only interpret the act as a desire for symbolic cleanliness. "Death no longer inspires fear solely because of its absolute negativity," writes Ariès, "it also turns the stomach, like any nauseating spectacle."[14] Rufi and I share the same mixture of fascination and disgust; our bourgeois senses are delicate. Rufi asks her mother what I, too, am thinking but dare not ask: How do you stand the sight and smell of death? Like her, I, too, want to displace the washing of a literal body onto some more palatable notion of a clean soul.

Polonia goes on to tell us that her mother had a prophetic knowledge of her death. She demanded that Polonia write to her husband in Madrid and tell him to come for the village fiesta in honor of the Virgin. Polonia recalled her mother's words:

"No, I'm going quickly. It's better that you call José. Write to José and tell him to come now."

"Look, mother, I'm not going to write to him because it's silly. Because you know he doesn't get much time off and then he'll have to leave. You stay calm, don't worry."

But her mother insisted. "No, you write to him and tell him to come for the fiesta."

"Why do you want him to come for the fiesta? We're not going to celebrate anything."

"Good, let him come. Write to him and tell him to come because I don't think I'm going to last very long."

The priest came to see her mother the day of the fiesta and he scolded Polonia for assenting to her wishes, because her mother didn't appear so ill. But when her mother died the night of the fiesta he admitted to Polonia: "That woman has made an impression on me. She seemed to have her days counted, she did. She knew that if she didn't die on the day of the fiesta that some time during those days she would die."

Rufi, who knew this part of the story, added, "It's that she had asked to die on one of the days dedicated to the Virgin."

At this point in the story all three of us paused, succumbing to the power of Polonia's mother's uncanny control over her own death, which had even surprised the priest. I, moved by this uncanniness, ask: "She wanted to die on one of the Virgin's days?"

"A day marked for the Virgin," said Polonia. "She had asked for it often. She would ask the Virgin, she was very devoted to the Virgin of Carmen. She had a book, with its worn pages, all worn."

I ask rhetorically, "Which she read?"

"Yes, she read it. She was very devoted. My father was the one who was very afraid of dying. He was very afraid, and it weighed on him a lot. He would say, 'Look, to have to die—' My mother had always subscribed to a magazine of the Sacred Heart of Jesus. And the mailman came, and one day he gave the magazine to my father there in the street. 'Here, have this, so you'll read it.' And he read a little bit of it. And he was reading, and he said that even with—I don't know how he said it. That with all the fun that we have here, that not even the best of times that we spent here could be compared to what takes place in the other world—dying in the grace of God. And he says, 'You know, I'm losing my fear of dying.'"

Rufi, shaking her head, says, "Ay, poor thing."

Rufi finds this all charming, folkloric, and sadly touching. She is at once attached and detached, close and distant, wavering between being close-up and taking in the scene with a telephoto lens. I find myself wavering in the same way between my ethnographic subjects and the family scene back home.

"'Well, look, if it's so good there, I don't know why we have to be so afraid.' I remember that a lot. 'And they're not going to treat us so badly, don't they say that God is all powerful, that he's our father?' My mother always said that. 'He's all powerful.' Of course, she would say, when she was already very ill, she would say, 'Not even Saint John the Baptist felt worthy enough to touch His shoelaces. How are we going to feel worthy to go to heaven and be the first ones there?' And she would say, 'Even though I think, you know, that I will be very well received in heaven. Because I have seven children there.' She had the sense that she had seven children in heaven."

I ask, to punctuate, "Because they died?"

"Because they had all died little, very little. And she would say, 'It's that I have seven children there. How are they not going to receive me well? They have to receive me well.' And I would say, 'Of course, and you know what father says, you've already read it.' I would say, 'Even the best times we spent here, it's even better what we will experience there.' And she, 'Yes, yes it's true. We say that, but how serious is the journey we have to go through.'"

For Polonia's mother, death was a journey. She hoped to be received well at the end of it; she even expected that she should be received well because seven of her children, sinless and therefore angelic, were already in heaven. Her father had more doubts, but he too, after reading the magazine of the Sacred Heart of Jesus, learned to repeat over and over, to convince himself, that there is another world and that the next world is better. Yet even with their doubts, the language of salvation and God's Kingdom was not an absurd language for them, nor is it even for Polonia who can still tell the story with pathos. For Rufi, however, this religious language is at best a quaint form of self-deception that only makes sense when it is displaced onto a distant rural past. Rufi's denial of coevalness with her grandparents seems too brusque to me. I want her to be less of an ethnographer and more of a granddaughter. I wish she wouldn't turn the stories about her grandparents into folklore quite so readily. She seems moved by death in general but not their deaths. Yet I realize that, like her, I find no easy way to redeem death. It is an ugly story of the body's deterioration. My grandfather is dying as I listen in the afternoon quiet to Polonia telling us how her mother died, and I realize I am not there with him. I have chosen to be at enormous distance, to hear how others die because I have not resolved how to be there with him. (Or, is this what I think now, two years later?)

"And she never let us stay with her. Later we brought down a bed for her here. Because she had a lot of trouble going up the stairs. And she would say, you two [Polonia and her sister], be calm. You two go to sleep calmly and don't worry. When I see that you need to spend the night with me I'll let you know. 'But mother, what if we don't hear you, what if you call us and we don't hear you?' Because of course with all the washing that had to be done, out in the well, with three children. . . . But she wouldn't let us stay with her. No, no, no, no. And you know what, the day that she died, in the afternoon, just at dusk, she said to us, she said, 'Tonight, you can't go to sleep, one of you has to stay with me.' And at half past three in the morning she died."

Polonia's eyes have filled with tears. A chill rushes down my spine. Rufi exclaims, "*¡Hala!*"

P olonia's mother not only foresaw but staged her own death, dying the "oldest form of death," the tame death that Ariès characterized as a sense of death as "close and familiar," in contrast to our sense of death as wild, "as so terrifying that we no longer dare say its name."[15] To await death peacefully, at home, in one's own bed, is no longer an option for people from Santa María. Now it is a sign of status, of being modern, to die in a hospital. Not to do so is strange, primitive, stingy. A dying person is no longer allowed to wait patiently in bed, rosary in hand, for death to come, surrounded by kin, neighbors, the priest, Christ, and the Virgin. This is what backward and resigned peasants did in the old days. The modern death is not a clerical death but a medical death.[16] One must take action, seek out doctors, spend money, and above all struggle against death, challenging any prophetic knowledge of its coming. I make these remarks after hearing Leonardo's story about Ramona's death.

I had put off going to talk to Leonardo Mirantes about Ramona's death. On a rainy day we sit talking in his dark kitchen. After talking about death customs in general, I ask, "So Señora Ramona died in León?"

"Yes, in the Princess Sofia Hospital. There she was for twenty days or so. She had been at home too, very ill. But the doctor wouldn't send for her. She had too many complications, who knows what. Then we had to take her at the last minute. And—One is always left with something. What if they were not attended well, during those days of the strike [at the hospital], who knows what? Death always has something about it—One is always left with something."

The reluctant ethnographer, I ask, "But later did you bring her back and have the wake for her here?"

Leonardo answers first by evading the question. "It was a fabulous funeral. A lot of people came. Many, many, many. They had to take me out of there, because I had an attack of nerves. They brought me to the church. So many people. It was Good Saturday. She died on Good Friday in the morning. That day Nieves [his sister], Margarita, and Ricardo [his daughter-in-law and son] went there to arrange things. Should they bring her, should they not bring her? And I said, 'If you want to bring her, then bring her, she has always been at home. But you know, she's here, and I don't see well. A lot of people have to come. And where do I receive them all? . . .' Well, since there was a chapel in the hospital they left her there. And they were there all day."

Rarely is the body brought back from the city of León before the funeral. All-night wakes in the village are infrequent; the last one I saw was in the early 1980s when Licorina, an elderly widow, had, like Polonia's mother, a prophecy of her death and demanded of her daughter that they leave their apartment in Gernika and return immediately to Santa María, so she could die in her house and in her own bed. Wakes are now held in the hospital chapel and then not all night, but for certain hours set by the hospital, and without the presence of the deceased.

"It's all sad. When we went she was in that place where they put them so they will be conserved. And they said that we couldn't—'Excuse me, listen,' said Ricardo, 'Please, it's that a sister who comes from such and such a place and comes all the way from Teruel and they have to leave this evening.' They say,

'Well, just for a moment.' Then they opened the door to what they call the freezer. And we all went in. We went in. Nothing. Me just a little bit. I reached over to touch her and she had a handkerchief, not a handkerchief but some rags, wrapped around her mouth. It's clear that when what she had inside burst through she spit out water from her mouth. And I tried to go towards her to kiss her, but I hit against the glass of—well, I wasn't doing well then—of the casket."

Leonardo's alienating moment of sorrow reflects how the hospital, rather than the family or the community, now takes possession of the dead. He was not present at Ramona's death and it is only by virtue of his son's insistence that the immediate family is able to enter the vault to attempt, vainly, to make a last contact with Ramona. His frustrated efforts to touch Ramona's body contrast with the intimate last washing of her mother experienced by Polonia, which Rufi finds strangely indecent.

"We often used to say to one another that if we both died at the same time, how happy we would be. 'If you die before me, what will become of me?' she used to say. And I would say, 'By right I should die before you, because I'm four years older than you.' And look, she died first. But we didn't think she would die. One never thinks of that. . . . Nowadays everyone feels that such things [illness and death] are better handled outside the home. And afterwards you always hear things said, that they didn't attend to her well, and so on. . . . These things that happen. Sad. But may God have received her in heaven." Leonardo's voice breaks off as he begins to cry. Modern death encodes a double sadness: grief stems not simply from the loss of one beloved, but from a consciousness of defeat—the sense that more could have been done, that the struggle ended too soon. We seem to grieve as much for the defeat as for the personal loss.

To quiet our emotions, we start talking around death and turn our conversation toward funeral homes and their key purpose of bringing the dead—more scattered, more distant now than before—home again for burial.

"If I go, for example, to the United States and die there, I have a policy that the funeral home has to bring me back. And they would say to me at the funeral home that, of course, some die a normal death at home and in those cases the funeral home ends up making a profit, but not with those who die far away. They told me that not long ago they brought someone back from Germany and that it cost 500,000 pesetas to bring him embalmed and in an airplane."

The bodies of those who have left the village to work elsewhere return by modern transportation, in the same way that they left, but they return, inevitably, to their village cemetery. It is the funeral homes that are entrusted with the task of returning the deceased to the village, circulating the news of the death, and handling the funeral and burial. Virtually every elderly villager, and many younger village migrants, pay a monthly fee to one or another funeral home in anticipation of a death that is expected to take place in a hospital bed or in a distant city. Dying takes place outside of the village, yet the final resting place is still the village cemetery.

We go on to talk about the death of Leonardo's parents, both of whom died at home. Leonardo described the old clerical form of dying. When a person was in his or her last agony, the family would call the priest, and immediately the bells would be rung in the particular way that signaled to the village that one of their members was about to receive the last sacraments. At this sign, a spontaneous procession would assemble, consisting of the priest carrying the chalice with the Eucharist, the sacristan carrying the crucifix from the main altar that accompanied all of the dying from the moment they breathed their last to the moment they were laid to rest, two men carrying the lanterns that were used in all the processions, and women bearing lit candles. In the company of Christ, the priest, kin, and neighbors, the person could "die well," taking leave of life in the grace of God.

The priest was a major actor in the final scenes of death when it used to take place at home. Stories are told of the faithless asking for last communion in their final hour, and many people still associate the approach of death with the presence of the priest.[17]

"Here the first thing you did when someone was gravely, gravely ill was call the priest. Grave, grave, then the priest. . . . And the priest himself, when someone was ill, he would go and make a consolatory visit, to cheer up the person. Now, I don't know. Since everyone dies far from home. Because in the past everyone died at home. The saddest thing was after working so hard and with so many children, so much of everything, and then to go die in a hospital. We thought going to the hospital to die was the worst thing imaginable. Now, on the other hand, it is the most common thing. Now few die at home. Unless one dies of a heart attack, of something while at home. But because of illness, very few. Because before then the first thing the local doctor does is send you to León, to the hospital."

I ask to underline the point about the priest's absence in the scene of modern death, "So now when one is sick one no longer calls for the priest?"

"No, no. Man, I don't know. Honestly, here we never called the priest, because she was never gravely, gravely ill. But during those days when she was like that, I never remembered to call the priest, nor did she. The doctor, yes. But the priest, not like in the past—Now the priest comes, and what is he going to do? Only—I don't know, those who have more faith perhaps call him. I don't know—Look, life ends" (*Mira, que se acaba la vida*). Leonardo's voice trails away.

In a conversation I had with Don Carlos Santos, a middle-aged priest from the nearby town of Boñar, he spoke with distaste for what he characterized as the emotional funerals of the past. "I remember during my first years as a priest in these lands, funerals were something truly, I don't know whether to say macabre. To me it was reminiscent of those images from there in Palestine, those Andalusian chants, those screams, those things: very lugubrious, very sad, and lacking in hope." Orientalizing the funerals of the past, he went on to note with satisfaction how "today, however, funerals, especially in Christian base communities, even if they haven't reached the ideal that we ought to strive for, are a celebration within pain, joyous of hope in Jesus. . . . The celebration of a funeral today is much more in keeping with the gospel and Christianity. And I think it more beautiful because of that." To learn to celebrate rather than mourn death has long been an essential teaching of the Church, but priests like Don Carlos seem to want to insist on this point in a way that virtually denies death. "In a funeral, what is it we do? Well, listen, we pray for a dead person, we believe in the hereafter, we believe in eternity, and we pray for a dead person, no? But at the same time, and most fundamentally, we are celebrating. We celebrate the resurrection of Christ, in which we, too, want to participate, and in which we hope to participate. That is why we celebrate."

This insistence on celebrating death accentuates even further the priest's growing irrelevance at the scene of modern death, and it expands the distance between Leonardo's whispered

"Look, life ends" and the priest's buoyant "We are celebrating." The way in which Don Carlos disdains the emotionalism of the old ways of dying leaves little room for public mourning, before or after death. Grief is forced to recede into the private corners of the psyche. It is no wonder that Leonardo and Ramona forgot to call the priest.

Ariès has noted how after Vatican II extreme unction was reconceptualized as the "anointing of the sick." The key sacrament which had, for centuries, made the priest a major actor in the moment of death was suddenly detached from death. "The clergy finally had had enough," writes Ariès, "of administering to cadavers . . . and finally refused to lend themselves to this farce, even if it was inspired by love."[18] No longer is it necessary or even truly possible to call in the priest at the moment of death, for the Church has bowed to the doctor in its desire to be absent at the moment of death. What is more, people no longer believe that there is anything the priest can do at the moment of death. Of course, though, as Ariès wryly notes, death has also ceased to be a moment. As Leonardo remarks, at the first sight of any serious illness the sick are sent off to the hospital; there death is stalled as long as possible, until inevitably it takes everyone by surprise, arriving unwitnessed and in solitude.

The luxury of dying at home, in one's own bed, is allowed only to those who die suddenly. To die like Polonia's mother, knowingly, is to force an early admission of defeat; besides, it makes the family look bad, as though it doesn't care. For this exactly is the stuff of gossip; as Leonardo notes, "Afterwards you always hear things said, that they didn't attend to her well, and so on. . . ." I did not know it then, but later I would learn with what courage, determination, and stubbornness, bordering for my family on inconsiderateness, Zayde died in his own bed.

When Leonardo and others of his generation speak of the customs and traditions they grew up with, they treat them not as objects of nostalgia but as the symbols of their previous deprivation; they treat them as "other." Those, they say, were the customs of poor peasants of another era. The irony is that they themselves were those peasants.

One afternoon I spoke to Sixto Mirantes and his wife, Inés Rodríguez, about the various rituals surrounding death, all of which involved the consumption and exchange of bread, the centerpiece of the agrarian diet and the symbol of Christ's body. The holiness of even everyday bread in rural Europe has often been noted. When women baked bread at home they wedged the sign of the cross into the dough, baking into every loaf the death and resurrection of Christ.[19] And, in Santa María, the bread was linked, also, to Mary, for it was said of these huge round loaves, which weighed five pounds or more, that they were not to be placed upside-down because this hurt the Virgin.

Bread was made a part of death in two ways. While all village people were required by the community to attend the wake and funeral of their neighbors, the family of the deceased reciprocated by providing bread and wine for all the male heads of households to eat together in the village assembly house following the funeral. This consumption of bread and wine by male parishioners was followed by the recitation of an "Our Father." In this way, the consumption of a very real and very ritual meal in memory of the deceased was joined to the wish that God should continue to provide the living with their daily bread.[20] By performing a "rite of reincorporation" the community (patriarchally represented by the male heads of households) repaired the breach signified by the loss of one of its members.[21]

Women were key actors in a different set of death rituals, the weekly public rituals involving the "bread of charity" (*la caridad*), or "blessed bread."[22] The female heads of village households took turns bringing to mass every Sunday a small loaf of bread, which was given to the priest, and a larger loaf, which was blessed by the priest and cut up, so that all the parishioners might eat a piece at the end of the mass. Another ritual coexisted with this, called the ritual of "bread for the souls in purgatory" (*el pan de las benditas animas del purgatorio*). The woman whose turn it was to bring blessed bread to mass would, on the evening before, go around the village collecting pieces of bread from the various houses for the souls in purgatory. Following the mass, the bread was auctioned off and the money thus earned was given to the priest, for him to celebrate masses for the souls of all the village dead, to aid them in their progress toward the purification that would ready them for entrance through the heavenly gates. The same bread that had fed those souls in life thus fed them, spiritually, in death.

In the years of the rural exodus and the reforms of the Second Vatican Council, these rituals fell apart. With the rural exodus came the depreciation of everything having to do with rural life and rural traditionalism; with Vatican II came the idea that "anachronistic" religious customs could be changed or even eliminated to make the practice of the faith "more modern."[23] In the early 1960s the practice of having wine and bread in the village assembly after the death of a villager was abandoned, though for several years the male heads continued to meet after the funeral to recite an "Our Father" for the deceased. Then in the early 1970s, the rituals of blessed bread and bread for the souls came undone when the rotation was broken by one neighbor and the next neighbor would not take it up again; all that was left was the tray that the priest had set out on one of the benches in the church, where those who so pleased could leave a few pesetas as alms for the souls.

"It began with people not believing," Sixto explained. "All my life I heard it said about that soup [the pieces of blessed bread] that it had the power to pardon venial sins. You would pick up the soup—Afterwards we no longer did it. But those who came before us would take the soup and as they took the soup they would go on their way reciting an 'Our Father' . . ."

Inés continued. "They abandoned it all. The blessed bread and the bread for the souls. Before, every Sunday, if it was my turn to bring the *caridad*, I went around collecting for the souls."

"And you sold that bread after mass in the portal of the church," said Sixto. "After that there came a moment when it was no longer done and they would ask in the same way, but one gave money. Everyone gave what they wished."

At this point in the conversation Inés offered a sardonic interpretation for the dismantling of these rituals: "Tell me, isn't it true that once you're 'full' you don't want another person's bread?"

I pounced on this. "What do you mean by being full?" I asked.

Inés explained: "For example, in the past there was more hunger than there is now. And of course since many were poor and that bread was sold for very little money, well the poor person would take that bread for the souls. If instead of paying thirty pesetas for a loaf of bread, that person got it for ten or fifteen, well they made do. Because of course there was a chunk from one person, another chunk from another, another from the pueblo. But the poor person made do with that bread. But afterwards, you know."

"Afterwards came a moment . . ." started Sixto.

"When nobody wanted that bread," concluded Inés.

"And then there came a moment when some would take it, and you know what they took it for? To crumble it up to give to the calves. And that was when . . ."

Inés concluded again, "people said, enough."

For Sixto, the loss of the old customs began with "not believing." For Inés, the loss has to do with material prosperity and with the increased pride and arrogance that, as she suggests, leaves people feeling "too full" (of themselves) to accept another person's bread. Both agreed, however, that once the bread was going to feed animals rather than people, the customs became meaningless symbolically and materially, quaint anachronisms in a time of prosperity.

Even the souls of the village dead no longer wanted, it seems, to eat masses made from the bread of other families. Nowadays, whoever wants to have a mass celebrated in honor of a dead soul pays the priest for it; collective masses for the souls are no longer said, except routinely on the Day of the Dead and at the mass for the village fiesta. Yet purgatory is where the dead are thought to go—since it is said that most of us are not so good as to go straight to heaven nor so evil as to go straight to hell—so that masses for the souls, now more individualized, continue to be viewed as an offering the dead need.[24] Masses are now routinely "ordered" by family members in memory of family members. These masses for the family dead are known as "the obligations," for the living, constituted now as family groups rather than communities, are obliged to remember the dead regularly by purchasing masses in their honor.[25]

On a Sunday afternoon in July I talked about these issues with Hilaria Carral, who has just retired from farming, and her daughter, Maribel Llamazares, a physical therapist in her early forties who is single, devout, and a Catholic activist. I have known Hilaria and Maribel since my first visit to Santa María, when I lived at their house. Hilaria, with her husband, Balbino, appeared in the cover photograph of my book *The Presence of the Past in a Spanish Village*, poised before a hay cart. When they saw the cover, they said that they must look really poor to people in the United States. I had, indeed, chosen a picture of them in peasant guise, not one of them in their street clothes or Sunday best. Only as peasants could they fit into my argument, be made visible there. On the day we talked about the cover photograph, I took another picture, of Hilaria with my son, Gabriel, on her lap, as she took a break from the hay harvest, which this time had been done by machine.

Hilaria was clearing the lunch dishes, and Maribel was washing them. Hilaria began by telling us a story her brother had heard when he was an apprentice blacksmith, about a house in which strange noises were heard every evening. The women who lived in the house had a brother who had gone to Buenos Aires and never been heard from again.

"They ordered a mass to be said," Hilaria told us, "because they began to suspect that maybe their brother had died and was suffering in purgatory for something he had done and had no one to plead for him. And they went and ordered that a mass be said for him. And that disappeared. The noise. Uncle Tino used to tell that story."

In response, I ventured to ask the obvious, "If one doesn't think about the souls in one's family, they may be discontented?"

Hilaria replied, "Of course. They need you. They need for you to ask for them. And maybe you don't remember them. But your obligation, listen, should be to remember them."

"To remember them, even in silence?" I ask.

And Hilaria: "Without a mass, without anything. Nothing more. Listen, when I go to La Salguera and look toward the cemetery, I always recite an 'Our Father.' For the obligations I have there."

Here Maribel intervened in schoolteacherly style: "In any case, mother, one thing should be clear, eh. That even if individually we didn't pray for them, it is our obligation, our obligation as Christians, to pray for our dead just as we are under obligation to pray for the living."

Hilaria did not miss a beat. "Some say that we need it more."

Maribel, driving her point home, went on. "More than for the dead. But what I'm getting at is one thing. Even if we didn't pray, even if I completely forget about my dead relatives, they are not forgotten. Because every time there is a celebration of the Eucharist, prayers are said for the dead. And when these prayers are said for the dead, it is for all the dead who need them. It's not going to go to you, to you, but not to you. . . . In all the masses that are offered in the world, in all of them, there is a remembrance of the dead, for all the souls in purgatory or however you want to call it. In all of them. It is wonderful to go to mass. And what is more, I think it puny and wretched to ask, always, always, always, for *my* dead. Always, always, always, for mine, mine, mine, no. I think it is much more; its love and its value have to be universal. For the dead. For whoever needs it most. Whoever it may be. Whether for the living or the dead or whoever."

Hilaria, however, was not totally convinced: "But look, we have an obligation also, eh. With our family members. With everyone, but with our family members especially."

Maribel was getting frustrated. "Well, especially when you pray, if you say I pray for my family members, then it means that everyone must pray for their family members. Then we are praying for everyone. But I think that it has to be more universal."

This kind of conversation between mother and daughter, like that between Rufi and Polonia, points to some of the generational cleavages from which new discourses about death and dying are being forged. Influenced by post–Vatican II theology, Maribel redefines the terrain of Christian charity to include the dead and the living in a kind of metropolitan City of God, an extension and urbanization of community and its traditional "bread of charity" or "blessed bread." This calls for a reconfiguration of the dead, even an erasure of the dead, who are depersonalized, rendered anonymous, stripped of their communal and family identities. Maribel's model is that of a welfare state in which spiritual aid descends upon those in need, living or dead, in a perfectly harmonious order of production and consumption. In this hypermodern vision of God's City, the remembering or forgetting of family and community no longer matters, because the individual, more alone now, is a citizen of the world.

Yet Maribel's vision is contested by her mother, Hilaria, who offers the village perspective on these matters: that one can and ought to apply masses specifically to one's own kin rather than universally and anonymously to all of those in need, and that masses are, in practice, appropriated, briefly becoming the private property of their purchasers. Hilaria, like Sixto and Inés in the previous conversation, is ambivalently critical of the increasingly commercialistic mentality that prevails among herself and her neighbors in the village. The same arrogance that leads people to feel "too full" to eat the bread of their neighbors leads them, too, to mark off particular masses as theirs alone to consume. Maribel interprets this desire to recognize only one's own dead in the sacrifice of Christ as a puny and wretched egotism that runs counter to the Christian message. Furthermore, to her purist sensibility that refuses to take note of the social construction of religion, the mass is the mass, no matter whether it is directed to a particular soul or paid for by a particular person. It cannot be bought or sold. Yet, to her mother, the universalistic thrust of Maribel's interpretation of the mass, while meaningful in the context of a universal church as social worker, is clearly alienating. Who will remember you if not your kin?

Hilaria now moved the conversation toward an issue that had clearly been bothering her. "It may be for everyone. But I direct them more for my own. I don't know if these are manias or what, but here you hear, constantly, a mass for so-and-so, a mass for the obligations, a mass here and a mass there. I say to myself, the person who orders the mass must be more worthy than the person who goes to hear it."

Maribel, ever anxious to correct village misunderstandings, was ready with an answer. "No, mother. The mass doesn't gain any value because you pay for it."

"I go to mass and I offer it," said Hilaria.

"Let that be totally clear to you, exactly that," replied Maribel emphatically, as though correcting an errant child.

"So-and-so ordered it. And will pay for it. But if I hear it, I offer it for my own."

Maribel, realizing that her mother had not yet understood her lesson, offered this explanation: "Look, mother, if I were to say I am going to give Don Laurentino [the parish priest] three thousand pesetas a year. Use them however you wish. And say he didn't offer any masses for the dead or for the obligations or for the living or for whoever you like. And he didn't make any offerings even though I had paid. And I go to mass and I remember them. That has just as much or more merit than if I go and, as you say, pay Don Laurentino for that mass. Let's not confuse things. Our ideas have to be a little clearer, eh. If not it looks like you are giving, paying. As if with two hundred pesetas you could buy a mass."

"Well, here we do believe that," said Hilaria crisply.

I, feebly joining in, "That you buy a mass?"

"That you order them for yours."

"But the mass is the mass," said Maribel, raising her voice with increasing irritation. "And the mass has the value it has. You don't give or take anything away from it by paying or not paying. You don't take anything away nor add anything to it."

I am not sure how to position myself in this conversation. I understand Maribel's desire not to want to commodify the mass. Yet I also understand Hilaria's feeling that the mass, like a glance toward the cemetery, is a memory tool for restoring the connection to one's own ancestors. I lean more toward Hilaria, though. Maribel seems too patronizing, too ready to analyze and correct her mother's ideas, too sure of the correct way to be a Christian. I have the same dilemma with Maribel as I have with Rufi. I should identify with them as someone closer to their generation, but instead I want to take the side of the older people. I feel a real loss in the refusal of Rufi and Maribel to accept the knowledge their mothers want to hand down to them. Their ethnographic distance is an exaggerated mirror to mine; I want more attachment from them.

On the one hand, Rufi's charmed fascination with the folk-loric, but distant, past; on the other, Maribel's ethic of forgetting, which obliterates memory and even the effort to remember.

Out by the rye fields just beyond the edge of the village is the little cemetery. I went there to see the niches that I had heard so much about. I was taken aback by what I saw, and the keen irony of the remark Angel Mirantes had made about their tombs being all that was left to the elders of the village struck me hard. With what seemed harsh and almost grotesque realism to me as I tried that summer to look away from death even as I thought about nothing else, people in Santa María had readied themselves for their tombs.

The niches form part of a massive cement structure built at the edge of the cemetery. While people pay the funeral homes precisely so that after death they will be sure to be laid to rest on native soil, the new burial setting they have created for themselves will no longer return them, in any real sense, to the soil. Radically departing from the local burial settings of the distant and recent past, people decided two years ago to construct *nichos*, in the village cemetery. To me the structure of "niches" looked like a very big file cabinet, but without the drawers. It has an apartment-like, cubicle-like feeling to it. For village people, the niches seem modern, in keeping with the times, like the pisos or apartments their children own in the cities of León, Madrid, and Gernika, except that they will occupy their "apartments" after death. There are thirty-two rows going across horizontally, each three niches high. With its gaping square holes waiting to be filled with coffin-drawers (only three holes have been filled so far), this prefabricated dwelling for the dead has (to my eyes) an amazing anticipatory quality.

The creation of this burial structure, which is becoming popular in many of the villages around the city of León, is the result of several years of discussion and argument in Santa María about the disorder and chaos in the cemetery. In the past twenty years, massive family tombs made of marble or granite, placed every which way, had begun to proliferate in the miniature cemetery, producing sometimes bitter competition for space. These tombs bore witness to the influence of urban notions of space, of nuclearized family living, and of the denial of death. The plots on which the tombs were placed were bought, becoming the private, and permanent, property of the family that purchased them. Previously, burial space had always been temporary, a part of the collective web of use-rights under which all property was subsumed; after five or ten years, grave plots would be opened, without ritual, and the bones transferred to the edge of the new grave, in this way constantly recycling very limited sacred space and communalizing the particular identities of the dead.

The niches represent a departure from both the family tomb and the recycled grave plot, and, in some ways, are a compromise between the two. On the one hand, they allow for an individual, permanent, and private burial space for each person; and since the niches were acquired in groups of three, they allow, too, for family unity at death. On the other hand, the niches are all exactly the same, making the sort of competition that had existed previously with the family tombs more difficult; and they were distributed in the traditional, egalitarian manner used to parcel out the common lands as well as the family inheritance: by lottery.[26] Even village factionalism has been memorialized in the niche structure, which was divided into two sections, with each faction hiring its own mason to do the work. Everyone now has a final resting-place ready. Laughing, Inés put it this way: "We each know which is our niche. We already have our house built there."

What strikes me as radical about the niches in the Santa María context is that they are a cruel symbol of finality, of death not as the regeneration of life but as the end of life, in this case the end of a particular, agricultural way of life.[27] The niches seem to embody a collective realization that a continuity has been broken; that there won't be a next generation to gather the harvest. Like city tombs that one pays to have taken care of, these niches will require no looking after, because weeds will not grow around the tight cement spaces; the living will more easily be able to forget about them.

I am stunned that the peasant bodies of the people I have known in Santa María will not return to the soil. The refusal to return the body to its original elements breaks with the agrarian view of death, of returning to the earth as the source of all regeneration. Yet I have to admit that my friends in Santa María seemed totally unconcerned about this issue. Were the niches enough of an imported status symbol—urban, neat, clean, ready-made—that people no longer cared where their bodies went? Or did I recoil from the niches because they seemed so alien from the Jewish perspective of creating as few obstacles as possible between the dead and the ground to which we must return? I know that the glaring otherness of the niches brought home the meaning of Zayde's impending death, from which I felt I had turned away. But I was also struck by the way this cement structure so pregnant with a collective readiness for death was a strange kind of monument—a self-chosen monument—to the awaited passing of the last villagers who stayed behind to till the soil. It seems to be a monument to the replacement of earth by cement and all that represents, of the village replaced by the city, the rural by the urban, bread by money, fertility by capitalism. Yet . . . is this my truth or theirs? Moved by duty-memory to not forget, have I encoded another way to brake, or at least mark, the acceleration of history?

On July 14, 1987, I woke up ill and nauseous with pains in my bones. But I had made a noon appointment to chat with the priest in Boñar and dutifully went to hear him speak of how death ought to be celebrated, words which I did not believe. On that day, five days before I was due to leave Spain, my grandfather died in Miami Beach. My father broke the news to me: "*Tu* Zayde passed *the way*." I spoke to my mother on the village phone, her voice quivering across the seas. "*Trató de esperar. Trató, pero no pudo. Trató de esperar por ti*" ("He tried to wait. He tried, but couldn't. He tried to wait for you"). The wind blew the phone wires. My mother's voice came and went, like waves fleeing and returning to shore. I picked up pieces of what she said. My poor mother. She herself had not arrived in time to see Zayde. "*Estando cerca, tampoco lo pude ver*" ("Even being close, I did not get to see him"). Dutifully, she had tried to finish up her work before taking a leave of absence; then, leaving at the first sign that Zayde was nearing death, her plane had been delayed several hours, and when she arrived, they had already taken him away.

I tried desperately to find a flight that would get me back in time for the funeral, but there wasn't one. Knowing that I would arrive late no matter what, I decided to wait until my departure the following week and then go straight to Miami Beach, to arrive for the last day of the *shivah*, the seven-day period of Jewish mourning.

During those days following my grandfather's death I hated myself for not having stayed in Miami Beach to help him die well, for having cowardly and ambitiously given priority to work over feeling and love. Instead I had gone to Spain to hear the death stories of my Spanish friends because I had not wanted to face the fact that Zayde was dying. I cried in my solitude, but found it difficult to mourn alone. Breastfeeding my little son, who would soon be a year old—Why, why couldn't Zayde have been allowed to wait for his first birthday?—I felt that he was sucking tears, not milk. My head swirled with different memories of Zayde: how, when I had seen him two months before, he had told me about a nightmare he had around Passover, when he dreamt he was a slave in Egypt and had to climb to the sky without any help; and how, several years ago, on a trip to Israel, he had gone to the Wailing Wall and crammed a piece of paper between the stones with a wish written on it: to live to 100. Memories lost to me of childhood closeness that photographs had preserved seemed, almost, to come back. I wanted to say the mourner's kaddish, to perform some sort of ritual for Zayde, but the truth was I was totally ignorant of Jewish death customs (later, I learned that the kaddish is not recited alone, nor is it recited for grandparents). Somehow, I had never been present at any death in my family; fate had spared me by leaving me in ignorance.

My paternal grandmother had died six years before, also when I was in Spain doing fieldwork. On that occasion, I did not get the message until several days after her death (there was no phone in Santa María yet). Wanting to take part, somehow, in the mourning, I had hurried to the flower shop in León, wiring a fancy bouquet to New York, forgetting that this was the wrong tradition, that in Jewish tradition flowers are not given at death. Rather, ready-cooked meals and baskets of fruit are given to the mourning family, which must abstain from work, and donations to charities are made in the person's name; or, more recently, trees are planted in Israel in memory of the deceased (this being the most problematic of the new invented traditions because the trees that stand as "living memorials" to loved ones often stand on expropriated Palestinian land). Stones, not flowers, are placed on the burial monument to mark one's remembrance of the dead, stones that one gathers at the cemetery to show one has been there. My mother later told me that my uncle Enrique, understanding that I had translated poorly out of too-sudden grief, had put the flowers in water, because no one else had wanted to.

That summer my grandfather died, I asked myself, in grief and rage, what bizarre accidents of education, ambition, and stupidity had led me to know how to recite a rosary instead of a basic Hebrew prayer. As an anthropologist, was I not convinced of the relativity of cultural approaches to death, of their equal validity? Why not recite a rosary for him? Why not have a mass said in his name? Because I knew very well that for my grandfather (and even maybe for me) that sort of remembrance would have been a worse fate than being forgotten. I was jolted out of my intellectual complacency, forced to see that cultural forms run deep into the rivers of being.

Rufi let me stay in my room the first day, but later she insisted that I ought not to be alone. With sisterly kindness and impatience, she led me down to the kitchen and I sat there with her and Polonia and a neighbor. Polonia chatted about old courtship patterns. I enjoyed her presence as much as ever, but I couldn't get up the interest to do fieldwork; the ethnographer in me, who was wavering during that summer anyway, had now totally shut down. I tried at least to be polite and still be good company, but the rationale for my being there had vanished. The weather, in the middle of July, turned nasty: cold and windy. I went out to the countryside, took pictures of wheat being punched by the air. I was looking for mirrors of my sorrow.

During those few, seemingly endless days that I spent no longer able to do much of anything, I reflected on the terrible sense of loss that my grandfather's death had awakened in me. Together with the pain of having lost him, there was the pain of having lost so much of the culture and the history that had been part of his lived reality and that had not been passed on to me. I remember how he lay in an armchair the last time I saw him, already dying, in the balcony of his condominium, from where you can smell the ocean, reading the Torah portion of the week in Hebrew to himself. I realized that this was something I could not do, perhaps never would learn to do, for at best I could read and follow Hebrew, but had to glance over continually at the English translation to know what the words meant. Even though I had heard his memories, had taken down his life history, so much had been lost; there was so much I would never be able to connect with because it was no longer there to go back to.

Zayde was a Russian Jew, who as a young man of twenty-two had ended up in Cuba, arriving in 1924. He was one of many Jews from Southern and Eastern Europe who migrated to Latin America after the United States closed its doors to these migrants with the 1924 Immigration and Nationality Act.[28]

Zayde had left Europe to avoid serving in the Russian army; he was thereby spared the cruel fate awaiting his siblings and his mother, who was shot in bed by the Nazis. He thought he had bought a ticket to Argentina, where his sister was already living. But when his boat docked in Cuba he was given the choice of staying there or going back to Europe, so he stayed in Cuba; in any case, like many migrants of his generation, he expected, eventually, to get to the United States.

In Cuba, Zayde kept kosher at first by eating nothing but bread and bananas. After working on the railroad as a peon and peddling watches on the street, over time he became the owner of his own little lace shop in Havana, his Casa Maximo (Maximo was the name the authorities gave him when his boat docked in Cuba; his family name was Moishe Aaron). In between the railroad and the lace shop he met and married my grandmother, Esther Levin, the eldest daughter of a Polish family, who worked with her father to bring her mother and six siblings to Cuba; their wedding invitation, in Spanish and Yiddish, was conserved by Zayde in his plastic folder of memorabilia that also included his railway worker's identification. He was terribly hardworking; my mother says they rarely saw him at home, for he was forever in the shop, which occupied the bottom floor of the same building. Then, after the Cuban revolution in 1959, he ended up in New York, and after retirement, in Miami Beach. In New York and Miami Beach he no longer had his own shop, but he continued to work selling fabric and lace in shops owned by other younger, more prosperous Cuban Jews.

He could never get over the fact that people made enormous profits in America; capitalism seemed to amuse, mystify, and alienate him in turn. Time and again, he would tell the story of how upon arriving in Cuba he tried peddling watches for a few more pennies than they cost him and sold nothing; then, at the advice of an experienced friend, he priced them at an outrageous ten pesos and sold them all in a day. His friend explained that if he sold the watches too cheap, then people thought they were cheap watches, but if he sold them dear, then people thought they were good watches; this friend also told him not to return to the same block to sell, for there were bound to be unsatisfied customers! In the United States, Zayde found humorous the huge signs in shops saying SALE (in Spanish "sale" comes from *salir*, meaning "to go out"), and he would speak cynically of these so-called discounts, saying *";Sale! ;Sale! No te preocupes. Todavía ganan"* ("Go out! Go out! Don't worry. They still make a profit").

We always spoke in Spanish, in translation, because after a heart attack years ago he said he had forgotten his English. The languages closer to his heart were Yiddish, for speaking, and Hebrew, for praying. Yet he had his jokes, which were only tellable in Spanish, an unusual Yiddishized Spanish; actually, they were not jokes so much as questions, like *";Como andas?,"* which he would answer with *"Con los pies,"* or *";Como te sientes?"* with *"En la silla."* (*;Como andas?* here means "How are you?," and, literally, "How do you walk?," which Zayde answered, "With my feet"; similarly, *;Como te sientes?* means "How do you feel?," which puns well with *;Como te sientas?,* "How do you sit?," to which his reply was "On a chair.") He hated hypocrisy and detected it everywhere, from the way people dressed up to go to synagogue, to the way they came to visit him, to dispense with their guilt, once it had become known to everyone but him (so he dissimulated, anyway) that he was dying.

Zayde was conservative in his political and religious convictions, but at least when I was growing up he struck me as a more liberated sort of man than my father, who had very demarcated ideas of female and male roles. Zayde washed the dishes and set the table; he made his own breakfast, swept the floors, and was wonderful with babies. None of this was true of my father, who raised my ire throughout my adolescence by insisting it was my duty as a girl to serve him and my brother. I did have one major falling out with Zayde, and the words he said then stung very hard. It was soon after my graduation from college, and I had decided to share an apartment with David. My father was anguished and enraged, and declared me dead. And my grandfather said, "The worst thing was that she chose a goy." My love turned to hate then, and I rejected Judaism as patriarchal and racist for a long time afterwards. (This, in turn, took a toll on my early fieldwork; I turned away, studiously, furiously, from the study of religion, burying myself instead in the details of inheritance and land tenure: a glaring omission that marked a displacement.)

Zayde was a man of few words, and for most of his adult life I think he felt inferior to his brother-in-law, Moises, my grandmother's brother, who is at ease with words, money, learning, and modern life. Moises, much more liberal and assimilated than my grandfather, is a man of the world: he has taken college courses and eaten seafood. It was his brother-in-law, a contractor, who sold Zayde the modest condominium in Miami Beach. When I saw Zayde two months before he died he showed me the record he was keeping of deaths in the family, inscribing them in neat Hebrew letters in the last volume of his Torah books. We had been talking about Moises, and Zayde said: "*Y él se cree que soy muy bruto*" ("And he thinks I'm very dumb"). I felt a tremendous hurt there, a hidden injury of class, and it pained me. Who now, I wondered, would inscribe his name in the book?

F lying back to New York and then to Miami Beach, all I could think of was death: Zayde was dead. I felt angry and imposed upon that I could no longer speak of him in the present tense. As we drove to my grandparents' house, everything seemed ridiculous: the palm trees, the blue sky, the harsh, clear sunlight, the tropical heat. Zayde was lying underground somewhere. How was that possible? I knocked at the door of their house. My mother, my aunt, my uncle were there to greet David, Gabriel, and me. And Baba? In the dark corridor Baba, my grandmother, looked frailer, smaller; she herself had hardly eaten during the months of Zayde's illness, watching as he ate less and less, his skin shrinking away from his bones. I could not stop weeping when I put my arms around her. By the glass door of the balcony there stood a little table, covered with lace, and on it was a copy of the Torah and the Yartzeit candle, lit and burning, as it is supposed to be during the period of the *shivah*. Four large cardboard boxes had been placed against the wall, for my mother, aunt, uncle, and grandmother to "sit" *shivah*, perhaps the most important symbol and practice of Jewish mourning.[29] My uncle was unshaven; my mother, aunt, and grandmother had not gone outside since the funeral and they looked pale and old. The large mirror in the dining room was covered.

That night people came to pray and to accompany the family. Sweets, cakes, fruit, coffee, and tea were left on the table for people to serve themselves. I sat on one of the boxes for a little while, but my mother did not like me to do that because I was not mourning a mother or father, brother, husband, or son, so

I soon got up. On Yom Kippur she had always run out of the Yizkor service recalling the dead, because she said her parents were alive and she had no reason to mourn, or to call death upon herself or her family by being there. I shared her fear.

The following day it was time to end the *shivah*. The rabbi, who was from the same town in Byelorussia as my grandfather, came to the house at midday. We talked for a while, and then he asked my grandmother, mother, aunt, and uncle if they were ready to set aside their public mourning, for their private mourning would not end so quickly. They stood up. He told them to form a line and walk around the dining table seven times. As they did so, they all wept; it was such a simple ceremony, this encircling or binding of death and mourning, and heartbreaking to watch.

In the afternoon an unexpected visitor came. She was a beautiful, elegant woman with pale brown skin who spoke a lyrical Cuban Spanish. This woman was the nurse who cared for my grandfather during the last two weeks of his life when the family, scattered and convinced that life had to go on, found itself unable to cope with Zayde's deteriorating condition. My mother, who had been with my grandfather just before the nurse was hired, had been shocked that Zayde agreed to be taken outside in a wheelchair while still in his pajamas, and that he felt no embarrassment at having her change the diaper he by then had to wear. "*Ya no le importaba*" ("He no longer cared"). His decline was unspeakably hard for those who had known him to bear. It was the nurse, a stranger, whose Cuban manner was totally familiar, and who restored my grandfather to himself then—not I, not my mother, aunt, uncle, or grandmother. It was from her that I learned the story of Zayde's death, which she told with tears in her eyes. She spoke of my grandfather as Don Maximo.

Lovingly, she recalled the look of gratitude on his face after she bathed and perfumed him.

"*Aquí, aquí le tengo*" ("Here, here I have him"), she said, pointing to her forehead. "*Su pelo blanco blanco, y su piel roja roja*" ("His white white hair, his red red skin").

A few days before he died he was in a wheelchair in the living room, and my grandmother had bent down by his side and told him, with her usual eloquence, how much she had loved him during all their years together, how she had tried to do everything as he wanted, having him stay at home rather than go to a hospital, and that if there was anything else he wanted, to tell her, please. I learned later that Baba desperately wanted him to speak, to utter last words that she would be able to repeat and remember. But Zayde, who spoke little, and did not much trust words, said nothing; instead, he turned to her and gave her a kiss. That was his good-bye, *el beso de despedida*, his good-bye kiss.

After that he was in bed, half-awake, but at peace. On the last day, his pulse quickened, and my aunt, who had been by his bedside, remembered how his hand had been very hot and how it suddenly went ice-cold. My grandmother was in another room and the nurse called her: "*¡Ester! ¡Ester!*" She came running, but when they took his body away, she couldn't bear to be there; she waited on the balcony staring absently out at the electric clock inanely flashing the time and weather over and over.

The nurse, in telling her story, had gotten everyone else to tell theirs. All of us cried, and felt grateful that this stranger, like an angel, had descended upon the condominium in Miami Beach where my grandfather died as he wanted to, in his own bed. In my heart I thanked her for restoring my grandfather's dignity as he lay dying, by treating him not as a sick, worn man reduced rapidly to bony dust, but as Don Maximo, a person still worthy of respect and esteem.

In the summer of 1988 Zayde's tomb was unveiled, following the tradition of erecting, dedicating, and blessing the gravestone a year after death. I stared at the gravestone for a long time and had an urge to caress it as I saw my Aunt Ida do at my grandmother's grave several years before. But I resisted. Out of the wet dirt I pulled up a pebble and placed it on the marble monument to his name.[30]

I dedicated my book *The Presence of the Past in a Spanish Village*, which focused on the traditions and memories of those who were structurally in a grandparent relation to me, to my own grandparents. While my own motives were not altogether clear to me at the time, with hindsight I have come to realize that my quest to understand "the presence of the past" in Santa María was but another link in the parallel quest to recover my own, and my family's, past. My grandparents had always been, for me, a key link in this quest, because of their passage from the Old World to the New, in the course of which they became Spanish speakers yet managed to remain Jews. There was an even more direct link to Spain on my father's side of the family; my paternal grandparents, who also settled in Cuba, were Sephardic Jews from Turkey, descendants of Jews expelled from Spain in 1492. There is a town in western Spain called Béjar, and working in Spain for me was partly about a search for something vaguer than roots, for the roots had been pulled out of the ground long ago. It was about a desire for memory, a "community of memory" in which I might locate my own life story.[31] At home I had sought out such communities of memory by urging my grandparents when I was growing up to tell me stories about their past, and in Santa María, by seeking out the stories of elderly people and viewing the changes in Spain from their vantage point.

I was less interested in the stories of the younger generation of villagers who had left the village for the city, just as I took little interest in hearing the stories my parents or their generation had to tell of their lives in Cuba and of their emigration to the United States. This was narrow-minded of me, to be sure, and showed how limited a notion of communities of memory I had, but I was convinced at the time that only the grandparent generation could link me, two generations later, to a past that would otherwise be cast away in the wreck of oblivion. In this half-blind searching, I have to admit, there was a tremendous fear of death: fear of my own death (fear which I have also given expression to in the lines by Allon White that I use in my epigraph; he died at thirty-six of leukemia). Writing history from the perspective of those who are approaching the end of their lives seemed to me a way of extending those lives, of mourning and remembering their parents, grandparents, and great-grandparents, and of escaping and laughing at death.

Zayde, in particular, was a link for me to my own peasant past and to the peasant existence that was still a living reality in Santa María. He had large hands, thickened by work, like the hands of peasant men in Santa María. He had grown up in the countryside, in a small farming town. His passion was to work outdoors, to plant, rake, clear up; he liked to use his large hands, and had made several shelves for me, but, above all, he liked to put order in all things, just as village men in Santa María took pains to leave their meadows mowed to perfection. His austerity was very much that of the peasant, and reminded me constantly of the disdain for conspicuous consumption that I noted among the aging villagers of Santa María, who were also highly critical of the new materialism of their offspring and sometimes of their own, too. He had piles of new shirts, ties, and colognes in his closet that were still in their original wrappers; for his part, he was content to wear the same suit. Like many village people, he treated money as treasure, reminding me of how in Santa María all of Heriberto's money burned to the ground years before when his wife, unknowingly, put fire to the old straw filling of his mattress. Zayde had added a secret drawer to his night table, where he stowed money without telling my grandmother; after his death, she found five hundred dollars in cash set aside for another great-grandchild he did not live to see, a daughter of my cousin Danny, born a week after Zayde died. I think my adoration for Zayde stemmed in large part from my sense that he was outside the acquisitive mentality that seemed to have engulfed the rest of the family; and I suspect that, similarly, what drew me to the older generation of villagers in Santa María was a sense that their attitudes and style of life reflected a submerged critique of capitalism, or at least a self-consciously embattled relationship with rampant consumerism and the idea of money as an end in itself.

Do I romanticize? Do I take the concern for loss too far? The Old World was also a hierarchical world, a patriarchal world, tainted with inequalities and exclusions. And, in anthropology, the theme of the "vanishing primitive" is already a cliché. So must I plead guilty to the charges of writing an allegory of salvage, engaging in imperialist nostalgia, and not being able to get over a sense of loss?[32]

This essay remains stubbornly mournful, a touch too morbid. Yet it is not about loss as a dreamy-eyed, or imperialistic, desire to bring back the past or to argue that things were somehow rosier before; rather, my effort has been to mark the fact of loss, and to show that there is an emotional force to this fact that we ought not to hide ourselves from. I want to suggest that anthropologists, and other vulnerable observers, can and should write about loss. But we must do so with a different awareness, an awareness of how excruciating are the paradoxes of attachment and displacement. Above all, I think we need to be absolutely pitiless with ourselves.

This essay tells two stories. It is a lament about death, loss, and grief, inscribing my mourning, a double mourning, as an anthropologist and a granddaughter.

But it is also about the effort to remember, and the need to remember, *my* effort and *my* need to remember, compelled as I am by duty-memory. Memory, however, is volatile, slippery; we tie it down, as the classical orators did, by linking it to places, sites. Thus Pierre Nora writes of "sites of memory" (*lieux de memoire*) that have become crucial in our time because of the sense "that there is no spontaneous memory, that we must deliberately create archives, maintain anniversaries, organize celebrations, pronounce eulogies, and notarize bills because such activities no longer occur naturally."[33]

Sites of memory operate in yet another way in this essay, which moves, as I did, from Miami Beach to Santa María and back again to Miami Beach. Here I have in mind the first epigraph: de Certeau's analogy between birds that lay their eggs in others species' nests and memory as that which "produces in a place that does not belong to it." De Certeau writes, profoundly, of the elusiveness and mobility of the process of remembering and of the remembered thing itself, noting the existence of a "double alteration, both of memory, which works when something affects it, and of its object, which is remembered only when it has disappeared." Remembering is an act of "alteration" because the "invisible inscriptions" that make up memory become visible "only through new circumstances." As de Certeau adds, the movement of his metaphors capturing the movement of remembering: "Memory is played by circumstances, just as a piano is played by a musician and music emerges from it when its keys are touched by the hands. Memory is a sense of the other."[34]

The notion that memory—which is a form of knowing—always takes place elsewhere, that it is always "other," is at the heart of the reflexivity that defines anthropological knowledge. My grandfather's dying and death while I was in Spain brought home to me—because I was away from home—the profound emotional power of the situation of the peasant elderly in Santa María. I could share, with Leonardo, with Sixto, and others of their generation, the force of emotion that death and mortality evoked for them—what it meant to have so come to terms with the dramatic changes that had taken place in the Spanish countryside to build death houses for themselves that the next generation would not have to care for. By another movement of memory, my conversations about death with people in Spain heightened my memory of my grandfather and the ways links to his past had been severed. And my preoccupation with the death of memory in Santa María provoked a resurgence of memory, for me, about my own Jewish heritage and how I had become alienated from it. In the course of these movements and shifts of perspective, the boundary between social realms that are purely personal and those that are part of ethnographic fieldwork became blurred. My grandfather was subjected to my anthropological gaze while I was drawn close personally to the people of Santa María.[35]

The sense of my own uprooting contrasts with the "rooted-ness" that, until recently at least, characterized rural village life, and which I sought out and took great pains to highlight. Commenting on an earlier version of this essay, Jill Dubisch wrote the following to me in a letter: "It is a deeply felt tragedy for us as anthropologists when those communities as we have known them cease to exist, not because we lose our subject matter (we don't), but because we fear the total loss of that rooted and con-tinuous and meaningful life which we had sought outside our own. That may be why we feel these changes as more tragic than the villagers do. For you, this sense was heightened by the parallel loss of your grandfather and all that he represented."

Indeed, I had searched for rootedness elsewhere—as anthro-pologists and travelers, in their search for the traditional, the rural, and the quaint, have done since the colonial era—and, in-deed, I had felt the loss of the old rural ways of life, carnally rep-resented by village elders, as a personal loss. Yet when, finally, in writing this essay I positioned myself not simply as an adoring granddaughter but as a historically conceived person, I found that my own values and fears were closer to the younger emi-grant generation that I had tried to detach myself from initially; I reacted in the aloof, sometimes enchanted, sometimes critical, manner of Rufi, or of Maribel, to the discourse of my elders in Santa María, just as I did not share completely in Zayde's way of being a Jew.

The factors producing distance between the generations were different for Rufi and Maribel than for me; they had to contend with the dramatic transformation of a fascist, poverty-ridden peasant society into a democratic, commodified society, while for me emigration, Holocaust, and revolution had been the key transformers. The ruptures were different, but there were points of contact between us; we were each trying to find a way to position ourselves in relation to an older generation—with mediation by our mothers—from which we felt distant. And there was pain in that distance.

For the anthropologist, writing about death can be an especially powerful way to approach reflexivity. "Working out an anthropology of death," as Johannes Fabian suggested, "we strive toward a realistic consciousness of death—ours."[36] Turning to the process of bereavement, both mine and that of my subjects, I try to get closer to death, close enough so that death is no longer a spectacle.[37] But there is a snag: death is the most difficult subject to write about. One thinks here of the "miracle" of Holocaust literature, which is born of the realization that "the Holocaust demands speech even as it threatens to impose silence."[38] A similar challenge is posed when writing about the culture of terror, say, in Argentina, where the government destroyed the humanity of its enemies "through unspeakable tortures" intended to deny, as Judith Elkin writes, "the worth of the death people died and the validity of the life they had lived." Writing about terror in Argentina, Elkin took a stand about what she would write and what she would leave silent: "Here I should recount some of the abominable things they did to people's bodies before allowing them to die, but I cannot bring myself to put them on paper and thus perpetuate them."[39] For Michael Taussig, the Putumayo terror called for an opposing literary strategy: the naming, over and over, of the abominations done to people's bodies, so as to toxify and overdose the reader into seeing the absurdity of the rationalizing idioms (for example, debt-peonage, cost-effectiveness, labor control) that would silence any speaking about the culture of terror.[40]

Even "ordinary" death leaves us on the brink between silence and speech. This is why anthropologists have found it less unsettling to write about "how others die" than to wrench from the resources of their experience and language some sense of how the dying of others speaks to "how we die." The shroud of silence, after all, offers protection against having to name the unnamable, as de Certeau calls death.

As de Certeau suggests, we place the dying in the secret zones of institutions so that they will not interrupt the chain of production and consumption that keeps our capitalist cultures running: "In our society, the absence of work is nonsense; it is necessary to eliminate it in order for the discourse that tirelessly articulates tasks and constructs the occidental story of 'There's always something to do' to continue. The dying man is the lapse of this discourse. He is, and can only be, obscene. And hence censured, deprived of language, wrapped in a shroud of silence: the unnamable."[41] I think here of how I was told that "life had to go on" when I wanted to stay in Miami Beach and help my grandfather die rather than go to Spain. Yet clearly I myself had hesitated to interrupt my work; otherwise I would not have voiced my desire as a possibility rather than a certainty. But let me also try to make a larger point, about the way in which countrysides like Santa María have been conquered by the new discourses about death and dying—a conquest in which I am implicated by my own complicity with the view of death as absurdly "other." The idea of "a break between life and death," with death viewed as "a defeat, a fall, or a threat," and life viewed as "a conquering labor," takes off in the seventeenth century, de Certeau argues, "in order to make possible ambitious scientific discourses capable of capitalizing progress," which in the eighteenth century find new direction in "the will to occupy the immense empty space of the countryside."[42] When we refuse to speak of how we die in our writings about how others die, we collude in the silence that our society would have us maintain about death in order not to wake from its dream of an irrepressible conquering labor. We also maintain the fenced boundary between emotion and intellect that is the academic counterpart to the practices that make dying "obscene."

Kafka once wrote that he hungered for books "which come upon us like ill fortune, and distress us deeply, like the death of one we love better than ourselves, like suicide. A book must be an ice-axe to break the sea frozen inside us." As Alvin Rosenfeld points out, Kafka was spared the Holocaust, which has made us become readers on the defensive, wanting "to keep the seas of empathy inside us safely frozen a while longer."[43] In our age of "compassion fatigue," I think anthropological writing about death has to be, if not an ice-axe to break the sea frozen inside us, at least an ice pick to chip at the conventional forms of representing and narrating the encounter of the anthropologist with death. Chipping away, reconstituting the dialectic between silence and speech, we will learn to take the deaths that take place over there, across borders, as seriously as we take those that take place here, at home.

P ost script, 1989. I can no longer declare ignorance of death in my family. As I revise this essay one more time, I realize, profoundly, how the texts of our lives, like those of our ethnographic subjects, do not sit still. It is December 13, 1989, the last day of mourning for my paternal grandfather, who died last week, also in Miami Beach, where he had lived since my grandmother's death in Brooklyn in 1981. I was not as close to Abuelo as I was to Zayde, both because I saw him less when I was growing up (for complicated reasons having to do with my father's own ambivalent relationship with him) and because he was not especially given to self-reflection. I approached his dying and death with more distance than I did Zayde's. I felt sad about this, and a little guilty that I couldn't summon up the same depth of emotion for Abuelo. I couldn't help feeling that Abuelo had given his family little; though he was exceedingly kind when we went to see him, he never sent a birthday card, never called any of us. Of course, as an anthropologist, I knew, on one level anyway, that his age and cultural background played a part in his apparent distance from us. Like my elderly friends in Santa María, he expected to be taken care of in his old age; it was our responsibility to call him, to take him places, to remember him. He did not understand reciprocity. I knew all this. And yet, foolishly perhaps, it made me feel distant toward him.

Abuelo was jovial, energetic, and carefree. A thoroughly public man with a handsome chiseled face and winning charm, he spoke a very boisterous Spanish with the rhythmic cadence of Ladino, the language of the Sephardim. He lived out his last years, as he wanted to, at the Majestic Hotel on Ocean Drive, which faces onto the beach, a solitary old man with half a memory, a solitary old man in love with the solitude of the sea. He said the view reminded him of his childhood days spent swimming near the port of Istanbul. He refused to live anywhere else, not with his eldest daughter in Hialeah, nor with his youngest daughter in Brooklyn, nor with my parents in Queens; to the relief of them all, I think. The Majestic Hotel was where he had vacationed with my grandmother and it held special meaning for him. All he had to his name was a tiny room with a bed and a television and a few changes of clothes. He bought a newspaper each morning to know what day it was. When you saw him he always said, joyously rather than sadly, "Here I am, for as long as God wants" (*Aquí estoy, hasta que Dios quiera*).

When, in October of 1989, the hotel owner decided to renovate the Majestic he evicted Abuelo, who had grown thin and senile during the years of staring at the ocean from the hotel porch. My father and his three siblings had Abuelo taken to a nursing home. I suspected he wouldn't last long there, so far from the sea and so fenced in. At the home they gave him a check-up and the doctors found cancer in his bladder. He claimed to feel just fine. But several weeks later his condition worsened and he was taken to the hospital. He refused to eat, or swallow even a spoonful of juice, for close to three weeks. On December 5, 1989, he died in my Aunt Ida's arms.

I learned of his death that evening and hesitated to tell my mother whether I would be at his funeral two days later. I wanted to maintain my pristine ignorance a little longer. But I did go. His body had been shipped from Miami Beach to Brooklyn for the funeral service, "like cargo," my mother said sadly. I remembered my conversation with Leonardo about the shipping of Spanish bodies by the funeral homes to their village cemeteries. Abuelo would be buried in New Jersey, near my grandmother's grave, in an aisle reserved for men, next to an old friend from Turkey.

To my own surprise, I asked to see Abuelo in his coffin; as the lid came up, I expected his death face to be grotesque, but he looked beautiful and pure. During the service the rabbi spoke of Abuelo's smile, his *sonrisa*, the sense of carefree joy he radiated; and he recalled Abuelo's early years in Brooklyn as a worker for Goodman's Matzoh. He had little in the way of riches, said the rabbi, but he had the generosity of his temperament. Like any obituary, this was an incomplete portrait of Abuelo, and we all knew it. After the visitors went out the door, the rabbi asked the family to form a circle around Abuelo's coffin. He asked us to put our hands on the coffin. Then he said, "If there is anything you want to ask forgiveness for, or grant forgiveness for, this is the time to do it." That did it. With those words we all snapped to pieces. My father cried like a child. The tears streamed down his cheeks as I had never seen before. I knew he held a good deal of bitterness toward Abuelo, who had put him to work at an early age to support the family—Abuelo himself never worked past noon—making it necessary for him to go to night school, where he was unable to study architecture as he had wanted to. Abuelo had also been cruel in ways I would never know of, because my father refused to speak; there was too much pain. I, in turn, held my own bitterness toward my father; he had put obstacles in the way of my desire to study, and too often he had tried to clip my wings. When I saw him cry, I melted. I was crying, too, for the grandfather I would never know, and for the one I had perhaps judged harshly.

Later, at the cemetery, along with my father and my brother and other family members, I shoveled dirt, according to ancient custom, into Abuelo's grave (I was the only woman there who did this). A bulldozer set to work to complete the job for us.

When had this custom begun, I wondered. I looked around me: everyone had good shoes, good coats on. No one present was in a position to get in there and get dirty digging and shoveling. There was no link to the world of agriculture in our little group that stood waiting in the bitter cold while the macabre bull-dozing came to an end. At last the grave was filled. The rabbi recited the last prayer. Then he went to the mound of earth and set down a small nameplate: Isaac Behar.

CHAPTER 3

MY MEXICAN FRIEND MARTA
WHO LIVES ACROSS THE BORDER
FROM ME IN DETROIT

Marta and I live a half hour away from each other, but there is a gaping-wide border between the corner house she and her family are borrowing from her brother-in-law in Detroit and my two-story Victorian house in a quiet, tree-lined neighborhood of Ann Arbor. Neither of us ever pretends that this border is inconsequential. Yet the circumstances of our lives have brought us at once so close and so far, and within that space we have managed to build a friendship.

It is June of 1993, and I am preparing for a return visit to Marta's hometown in Mexico, where David and I have lived, off and on, for ten years. She herself can't go back, because her husband Saúl has just lost his job and their economic situation is shaky. So this year I will be the one to hug her parents and sisters, and to spend afternoons chatting in the patio with her *abuelitos*, her beloved and frail grandparents.

Marta arrives with Saúl to drop off a Sears catalogue for me to take to her family. And she brings their video camera to shoot some footage of my house. For Marta my house is a museum. She goes around talking into the camera as she points out highlights in our living room and dining room.

"We come to this house a lot. Our friends like to invite us over," she says, chuckling.

My house is filled with books, embroidered cloths, and antique furniture; and there are clay pots, enameled trays, and bark paintings brought from Mexico. It is a house of many rooms, wood-framed windows, and a garden. I sometimes can't believe it is my house, bought with my own money. As a Cuban immigrant kid, I grew up in a series of cramped apartments in New York, so when Marta tells me she loves to come to my house, that it is her dream house, I understand, but feel odd that the things I have acquired are inspiring wanting and longing in someone else. She takes notice of anything new—a wicker chair, a used piano, a Turkish beaded good luck charm, new tiles in the bathroom with whimsical nopal cactuses, also brought with us from Mexico.

Marta focuses her camera on all of my Mexican wares. "Look at all the beautiful things from Mexico," she says into the camera. She seems to be displaying for her family back in Mexico all the Mexican things the anthropologist has in her house, which the Mexican herself, namely, Marta, doesn't want to have. Marta, for whom Mexico is her grandparents, her seven siblings, and her mother and father, who were always working not to become poor, desires none of these things; she dreams of packages filled with pretty white linens, edged in lace, that you order from catalogues, and she wants elegant, gold-trimmed porcelain dishes, the kind you can sometimes find on sale for fifteen dollars, service for four, at Kmart.

I am always the one who phones Marta. When Marta decided to marry Saúl and come live with him in the United States,

I made a promise to her parents and grandparents in Mexico that I would always look out for her on this side of the border. I haven't been able to explain to her family that another border separates us here.

"Marta, how are you?" I ask in Spanish, addressing her in the informal *tú*. We have spoken our native Spanish to one another since we met ten years ago in Mexico. We may both speak English to our sons, but our friendship is lived in Spanish.

"I'm fine. And you?" Marta always addresses me in the formal you, as *usted*. She won't let me forget that I am ten years her senior; that when we met in Mexico she was a young girl finishing high school and I was already a married woman embarking on a career as an anthropologist and writer. Even after seven years in the United States, and my continual requests that she address me as *tú*, Marta insists on maintaining certain formalities that acknowledge the age, cultural, educational, and class differences between us.

"And how is Saúl?"

"He's okay. He got that job teaching high school Spanish. Says he's going to earn almost as much as he used to at his old job. Says he's looking forward to the long summer vacations. We're just waiting for them to call about his physical exam."

I have known Saúl for about as many years as I have known Marta. Born in the United States of Mexican parents, Saúl grew up in Michigan, working summers with his four brothers and their parents in the cherry, apple, and cucumber harvests. When I met Saúl, he was searching for his roots in the same Mexican town in which David and I were searching for a topic to study. He'd usually visit around Christmas, hosting lively *posadas* at the house of his mother's cousin, where the tamales were plentiful and a big piñata bulging with sweets was never lacking. On one of his first visits, when I met him, he came with a girlfriend, a *gringa* with long curly blonde hair; and years before, he had come with a different girlfriend, also a *gringa*.

But during the Christmas season in 1983, he came alone. Marta, who had won a scholarship to attend a state boarding school, was home on a vacation from her job teaching in a rural school. Her hair was permed, she wore a pink knit blouse and fitted pants, and danced an entire night with Saúl at a fifteenth-birthday party, the *quinceañera*, of a cousin. Soon after, when he returned to the States, they wrote letters to each other every day. Two years later, they decided to get married, against the objections of Marta's father. He described Saúl, thirteen years older than Marta, as a *gallo*, an old rooster, who wanted the hand of a *pollito*, a little chick.

Marta and Saúl were married in a big church wedding in Mexico in December of 1985 and moved to East Lansing, where Saúl worked in the personnel department of Michigan State University. In the university setting, Marta met other women from Latin America and studied English. Saúl, who realized he had taken Marta away from her job, hoped she'd prepare to become a teacher of bilingual education. But Marta soon decided she wanted to have a child and, without letting Saúl know, she let him get her pregnant. What she hadn't expected was that it would happen so quickly.

Their son, Eduardo, was born in 1988, when Marta was twenty-three, and in 1989 they moved to the Detroit area, where Saúl found a better-paying job in a state government office. For the next three years they lived in a garden apartment in Romulus, under the flight paths of the Detroit Metro airport, where few families with children lived. Marta felt unsafe and stayed indoors all the time, shut within the four walls of their apartment, with her baby and the television as her only companions. Marta says she learned English watching soap operas. Later they moved to another apartment in Westland, where there were more families with children, and the stores were within walking distance. It was not yet Marta's dream house, but at least she felt less isolated.

Then Saúl lost his job. To save money he and Marta gave up their garden apartment and moved into his brother's house. It was a difficult moment, especially because they had taken on the added responsibility of caring for Marta's brother and sister, who had come from Mexico with all their papers in order thanks to Saúl's efforts. Polo and Lisandra planned to complete their last year of high school in the United States and then study in a community college. The two of them had learned English quickly and progressed rapidly in their schoolwork. Saúl was proud of them and hoped their presence would cheer up Marta, who had grown depressed and moody in her new surroundings.

"Guess what?" Marta suddenly announces. "I've signed up for a course. Saúl says it would be good for me. It's a course about relationships, about letting go of the anger you've been carrying around since you were a child. Do you know I still have dreams in which I get angry because my mother isn't home to take care of me?"

Women think back through their mothers, and, indeed, Marta wants to become a different kind of mother than her mother. Marta tells me that her adult self comprehends that her mother had to work hard, first as a peddler and then as a school-teacher, to care for her eight children; but even so, she says with anguish, she can't forget how as a child she felt neglected and wished she could be wrapped inside her mother's arms, those arms which were always busy working. In the United States,

Marta imagined she could become the mother she didn't have, the mother who would plan her pregnancy and be exclusively devoted to her child. And so she chose to have one child, Eduardo, for whom she has cared singlehandedly during the early years of his childhood. And she has chosen, too, to make it impossible to ever have another child.

I t is October of 1992, five months after Marta's hysterectomy. With some hesitation I have asked Marta if I can write about her operation for a conference on women's health. I fear that treating her as an anthropological subject will hurt our friendship, but Marta immediately agrees to let me write about her. She considers it an honor, she says, that I am interested.

We sit on her bed with the white lace coverlet. A mirror is behind Marta and I try not to look at my own face as I look at her. Little Eddy is in the living room playing with David, who has accompanied me on this trip because I don't like to drive to Detroit alone. The tape recorder is on the bed and I hold up the microphone toward Marta. We don't know that the tape recorder is not recording anything; only later, when I get home, will I learn that David forgot to put the batteries in the microphone.

On three sheets of lined loose-leaf paper, Marta has begun to write her life story in a few broad strokes. I read her handwritten words and notice how careful she has been to leave out anything painful; but her sense of solitude is profound and it surfaces, unwillingly, several times in her brief text, which ends in mid-sentence, with the words, "I have tried not to be an abnegated wife, but a . . ." She has held within herself all the pain of social and cultural displacement, all the tension of her rite of passage from virgin to wife, and all the anxieties of losing her womb so soon after becoming a mother.

Knowing that she planned to have only one, or maybe two children of her own, Marta tells me she tried to enjoy every moment of her pregnancy. It was a special time that she remembers with joy. But giving birth was a nightmare for her. At the hospital, when she became fully dilated, the doctors told her that the baby's head was too big and that they needed to perform a C-section. They had given her a spinal block for pain relief and later they put her under total anesthesia to perform the C-section. Saúl was not allowed to be present at the birth and the staff delayed bringing the baby to her. Apparently the anesthesiologist was sloppy, because after giving birth Marta suffered for four months from terrible headaches and body pains caused by the spinal block. She cries remembering how she could barely take care of Eddy at first. For Marta, having a C-section, especially one that was botched and alienating, made her feel that her womb wasn't worth much. She told me that the doctor who took out her uterus cut along the dotted line of her C-section scar.

Marta found the doctor who performed her hysterectomy, a board-certified obstetrician, in the phone book. She had already gone to two other doctors, both women, before seeing him. The two previous doctors, she felt, were unscrupulous in their desire for money; after learning what a good health insurance plan she had through her husband's job, they had immediately wanted to perform hysterectomies without even running a single test or analysis. As a rule she prefers women doctors, she says, because she's a Latina and finds it shameful to be examined by a man. But the doctor she found in the phone book impressed her enough that she put her trust in him. He's Cuban, she tells me, which I already know, cringing at the thought that Marta, in a subliminal way, may have put her trust in him because she's learned from me that Cubans are okay. I am holding the microphone that is taping nothing as she tells me that she wanted to have tests done and the Cuban doctor did them. She wanted to be sure she needed this operation and he convinced her she did. Her heavy menstrual bleeding had worried her since she was a young girl, but after giving birth, it had gotten worse. She had to rest during her periods and take iron; during those days, she fell behind on the cooking and cleaning and she didn't like that, because if the house was going to be her only responsibility, she wanted to do it well. The doctor told her if she went on bleeding so heavily one day she'd have a hemorrhage. He also told her that she had a tumor in her uterus, but after removing the uterus he admitted there was no tumor. He claimed her uterus was abnormally enlarged, that it had not shrunk back to its proper size after pregnancy.

Marta is beginning to question her doctor's advice and motives. She is not so sure anymore that he wasn't out for the money, too. And she recognizes that he's not so honest, perhaps, as she thought at first. When she tells him she's been gaining weight after the operation, he pretends it is her eating habits that are responsible; but later she finds out that it's very common for women who lose their uterus to put on weight. But what matters is her health, she says. It's nice not to be worried about her periods anymore or about getting pregnant. She couldn't have gone on taking iron pills forever. And if she is not going to have any more children anyway, then she really doesn't need her uterus. She's lucky, she tells me, that Saúl is educated and accepts her in her new wombless state. In Mexico, she says, there are men who won't have a woman who's had a hysterectomy; they claim those women aren't women anymore.

Marta needs to affirm to herself that her decision was a wise one. She thought about it for a year and she feels she explored her options by getting several medical opinions. She believes her health has improved, that she is really better, much better. But the loss of her uterus has made her aware of all her losses—of everything she has given up, everything she is giving up, to make a new life for herself and her family on this side of the border.

Listening to Marta, I am remembering how, a few years before, in Mexico, I held the delicate hand of her wispy *abuelita* and promised I would do everything in my power to protect Marta from the many perils of modernity on this side of the border. Ay, how I fear that I have failed miserably to live up to my promise. And this anguish runs deep into my own life—Marta had her hysterectomy a year after my mother had hers. When my mother was trying to make up her mind, she asked me for advice. Her daughter, the professor, would surely be able to tell her whether she really needed to have her womb cut out. But at the time I was so pathetically ignorant I encouraged my mother to go through with the operation. Only later, belatedly, uselessly, did I acquire the cruel knowledge that in the United States more unnecessary hysterectomies are carried out than in any other country in the Western world. Had my mother's hysterectomy been unnecessary? I no longer knew what to think, but I experienced painful daughter's guilt, shame, and self-hate, wondering if my mother's body had been sacrificed, with my complicity, to the surgeon's knife.

When Marta let me know her plans, I became distraught again. This time, with Marta, I was in a position of knowledge, even of too much knowledge, about hysterectomies. And I shared my doubts with her, urged her not to make too quick a decision. But I also questioned my desire to intervene. Was that the role I should be playing in our friendship? Did I really know what was best for her? Marta had made up her own mind with a strange sense of rational passion and tragic inevitability. She seemed to be marking her arrival on this side of the border with truly brutal retribution—which, sadly, was directed at herself. All I could do now was mourn with her, mourn her truly unbearable losses, and in that way help her to heal.

You know, Marta says to me, the last time she was in Mexico she and her mother were joking around and her mother called her a good-for-nothing. Those words—"*no sirves para nada*"—stung, and the pain was compounded when Saúl recently said the same thing to her, also as a joke. As she recounts this, Marta's eyes fill with tears. Marta was the second daughter; it was her sister, the eldest, who was always the smart one, always the favorite of her father. When she was in Mexico, her father told her how proud he was of her older unmarried sister for having gotten so far in her studies and achieving degrees in two fields. But he didn't say anything to Marta about being proud of her. She longs for greater affirmation from her parents, and yet her deepest wish is to someday bring them both to the United States and provide for them in their old age.

Marta left everything behind to come to the States with Saúl, but she didn't receive a very warm welcome from his family. When her mother-in-law suddenly developed an inexplicable illness, her father-in-law accused Marta of having used witchcraft to cause the illness; later he told Marta that Saúl didn't love her and that she was lucky he had paid any attention to her. One brother-in-law called her an Indian from the *rancho* because she refused to drink beer; another brother-in-law told her she was "*un perro entrenado*" (a trained dog), because she was so concerned to keep Saúl happy, having dinner on the table when he returned from work and setting his clothes out for him, neatly ironed, each morning.

She doesn't do those things for Saúl anymore, Marta says, because he never thanked her, never showed any appreciation.

If Saúl thought he was bringing back a young and innocent Mexican wife to do all his housework for him, those days are over, she says, wiping her eyes, her face hardening.

As David and I drive back to Ann Arbor, I tell him about how Marta told me she often feels worthless, that her life isn't amounting to anything. Tears come into David's eyes; he says that's how he often feels.

In our relationship, the usual division of labor and power has been reversed. David has played the role of faculty wife, caring for our son, Gabriel, and doing the kind of secretarial work for me that male professors are always thanking their wives for in the acknowledgment section of their books. Most of the time, I am able to display gratitude for David's help on a more regular basis and to encourage him in his own work, but I have also been spoiled by the bargain prices he offers on his services; like my male counterparts, I've gotten into the habit of depending on certain unpaid labors from him. So, back at home, when I discover that the tape on which I am expecting to base my paper for the women's health conference hasn't come out, a paper that must be ready to present in a week, I break out in a merciless fury.

"Why did you give me that microphone in the first place? I've never used that silly thing before! How was I to know it needed its own battery? Aren't you the one who always handles that stuff? Now what am I going to do? I can't replicate the conversation I just had with Marta! I may as well forget about going to the conference. And my paper is one of the plenaries. Thanks to you, I won't be able to go!"

David's head sinks. "I'm sorry," he says. But I go on, repeating the litany of my complaints, even though I know I'll be able to piece my paper together from notes and memories. After a while he gets angry enough to say, "Well, next time, *you* get the tape recorder set up."

"That's very easy to say now, isn't it?"

"Look, if you don't like the way I do things, maybe I should just leave."

"You really love to press the anxiety button by threatening to leave just when I'm counting on you to take care of Gabriel. That's so cruel!"

In the afternoon the two of us go to our yoga class, where we pretend not to recognize one another and occupy different parts of the room as though we were strangers.

Sometimes anthropology comes too close to home.

A few days later we return to Marta's house with a functioning tape recorder. David goes off to look at computers and I stay with Marta and Eddy. Our conversation is not so intense this time because of Eddy's interruptions. At one point Marta takes Eddy in her arms and holds him tight. "I try to remember to do this at least once a day," she says. But later, he gets wilder, and trying to get her attention, he punches her in the belly. "I'll be right back," she says and goes into the bathroom with Eddy. I think I can hear her hitting him. Lisandra is back from her high school and comes in to entertain me. No, I can't believe she'd hit Eddy, her one and only. Would she?

Marta returns with Eddy and I can't read any clues in his face or hers. From the closet she pulls out her photo album, and we slowly turn the pages, looking at the pictures of her as a student, eyes gleaming with promise. Eddy points to a picture of Marta and says, "Stupid!" Marta calmly says to him, "Don't say that. Say chicken." Eddy points to the picture again and says, "Stupid!" Marta takes a deep breath and repeats, "Say chicken, Eddy, okay?" Her eyes look like they're starting to water. Finally, Eddy whispers "Chicken" and Marta says, "*Gracias*, that's better, Eddy."

Eddy soon tires of the pictures and rushes out to the living room to watch the cartoons on television. Lisandra, always good-natured, excuses herself and follows after him. Glad to be alone with me again, Marta returns to her closet and pulls out a stack of neatly folded, sparkling clean towels. "These are my towels," she says. "I don't let Saúl or my brother Polo use them. Polo has pimples and I don't want him staining my towels."

Then Marta pulls out a big plastic bag. It is full of letters, the love letters Saúl wrote to her from Minnesota, North Dakota, and Michigan in the two years of their romance. She reads from two of them: one letter is about his struggle to find work after deciding to leave Minnesota; the other is about how they should deal with the problem of getting married by the Catholic Church, given his family's conversion to Protestantism (but later, as Marta explains, it turns out that his grandmother had baptized him and there was no problem at all). He'd start his letters with *Amor mío* ("My love"), punctuating them constantly with those words. He wrote very lyrically and in correct Spanish. When he went to ask Marta's father if he would let her marry him, Saúl announced, "I have a great weight upon my heart," and her father said, "Forget the poetry and get to the point."

Saúl saved all her letters just like she saved all of his. But her letters are gone. Destroyed by her own hands. Why, I ask, unable to hide the disappointment in my voice. Marta says she just decided, one day, to tear them all up. She told Saúl she was going to do it. And all he said was, "Well, if that's what you want to do . . ."

B ack in a small town in Mexico, in the front room where her *abuelitos* sleep, Marta's wedding dress hangs from a nail in the wall. The dress remembers her body. Remembers how she danced before she said good-bye. Waits for her.

CHAPTER 4

THE GIRL IN THE CAST

Five persons were killed early yesterday when an auto driven by a newly licensed teen-ager hurtled a dividing barrier on the Belt Parkway at the Pennsylvania Avenue exit and landed on top of an auto going in the opposite direction.

The dead included four neighborhood teen-aged friends, who were riding in the first car and a 24-year-old Hofstra College senior, who was driving the other vehicle.

The police of the Miller Avenue station house in East New York said that the car in which the four teen-agers were riding was returning from a discotheque dance at Murray the K's World, a restaurant in Roosevelt, Long Island . . .

The car hurtled the center island divider, a foot-high concrete curb topped by a three-foot metal fence. It landed on top of an auto traveling in the opposite direction operated by Joseph J. Venturino of 46 Radcliff Road, Island Park, Long Island . . . With him was Miss Betty M. Saltz, a 20-year-old secretary employed by a motion picture firm . . .

Mr. Venturino, with split-second timing, swung his car to the right to protect Miss Saltz and took the full impact of the blow, killing [him] instantly and trapping his body in the wreckage. Miss Saltz was taken to Brookdale Hospital and held there after treatment for a fractured right leg and left collar bone and multiple lacerations. She was reported in fair condition.

Three other autos, driving behind Mr. Venturino's car, piled into the wreckage. In the first car, Albert Behar, 32, of 141–65 85th Street, Jamaica, Queens, was driving with his wife, Rebecca, 30, a daughter, Ruth, 9, a son, Maurice, 10, and Mrs. Behar's mother, Mrs. Esther Glinski, 60. All were taken to Brookdale Hospital, where only Ruth was detained for a fractured right leg.

—New York Times, May 1, 1966

The story in the epigraph, with the headline "Five Die in Crash on Belt Parkway," appeared on page 48, next to an ad for emerald rings and brooches at Bloomingdale's department store. What happened to the Behar family is a footnote to the story. What happened to Ruth is a footnote to the footnote.

After the accident my childhood ended.

I was told it was horrible. It was one of the worst car accidents in New York traffic history. The *Daily News* put the story on its front page.

My brother, who was actually six, not ten as the newspaper incorrectly reported, remembers seeing the car flying. It looked like it had wings. My grandmother remembers having to walk over dead bodies. My mother remembers that my grandmother kept screaming and screaming and clutching her heart. My father remembers stretching his arm across my mother's chest to keep her from crashing through the front window.

I didn't see anything. I barely remember anything. I was asleep on my grandmother's lap in the backseat. We were on our way home. When I awoke, I was all alone in the car. Where had everyone gone? I wanted to escape, too, but suddenly I could no longer walk. My right leg had swollen like a watermelon.

I heard my father's voice through layers and layers of distance. He was saying he had to get me out, that maybe the car would catch fire. At that moment, and this I remember vividly, I looked down at my left foot and noticed that my shoe was missing. It had flown out the window. What would I do now with only one shoe? I'd be sad like Cinderella. They were brand new shoes, black patent leather shoes with little black satin bows.

"Papi, my shoe—"

But my father didn't go and find my shoe. He picked me up and pulled me out of the car. That was when I noticed the pain. That was when I began to cry. At Brookdale Hospital I was wheeled into the emergency room with Betty Saltz. I cried and cried. A doctor there told me to be quiet already, that the woman next to me would be paralyzed for life, and that I should be happy I just had a broken leg.

I was not allowed to feel sorry for myself because it might have been worse, and I was not allowed to be angry with the young men who had caused the accident because they were dead. The adults kept telling me I should be happy.

Happy, happy, happy. It's just a broken leg. A femur bone broken in a few places, that's all. Imagine if the leg had needed to be cut off. Or, worse, what if I had ended up a vegetable? I had to be grateful.

And so the nine-year-old girl stopped crying. It was bad to cry when you were supposed to be happy.

I didn't cry when they wheeled me out of the operating room, reincarnated as a mummy encased in a body cast of thick white plaster. My parents thought the doctor had gone mad. So much plaster for a broken leg? Why hadn't he given me a walking cast? The doctor tried to explain in simple English that with a walking cast there was a risk of one leg growing longer than the other, leaving me with a permanent limp. He wanted to be sure my legs would grow at the same rate and the only way to do that was to put them both inside plaster. I was going to have to be inside plaster for a long time and he didn't want to take any chances. My parents were not convinced by the doctor's explanations, but they were immigrants making only enough to pay the rent, so what else were they going to do? Two years later, when I was fully healed, they would bless the doctor many times over, but they took home very reluctantly the girl in the cast.

The cast began just below my unformed breasts, took in my waist and hips, and enclosed each leg down to my toes, the tips of which stuck out like little fish coming up for air. A pole linked my legs at the ankles. With that pole, the doctor explained, my mother would be able to turn me on my stomach at night to sleep. My head and shoulders could be propped up with pillows when I ate, or if I wanted to read a book. The rest of the time I was to lie flat on my back.

Just below my belly an opening had been carved out for my private parts. Suddenly, the parts of your body you were supposed to hide, and that as a girl you were supposed to keep tightly locked between your legs, were wide open to view. With the cast, my legs were spread shamefully far apart and fixed in place. Nothing except the bed sheets covered my torso. I learned to pull the sheets up to my shoulders and cling to them tightly when other children were in the room, fearing that in cruel jest they would pull them off and leave me exposed.

I still had a young girl's body, but I already knew that within me there was a woman's body waiting to sprout at any moment, just when you weren't looking. My mother had shown me her box of Kotex napkins and explained to me that in a few years I would become a young lady. I think she must have also tried to explain that once girls became young ladies they could have babies. And she must have hinted at how babies were made.

I remember, though I couldn't have expressed it then, that my attainment of sexual knowledge became connected in my mind to the car accident. The accident happened on our return home from Staten Island, where we had visited my mother's cousin Alma, who had just given birth to her second child, Miriam. At Alma's house I remember I overheard jokes I was not supposed to understand, and they had to do with what women and men did and how when they did it they sometimes had babies. Something about these jokes disturbed me and scared me, but I don't know what exactly. Soon after, we said good-bye, got into the car, and I fell asleep on my grandmother's lap. When I awoke I was a cripple.

For the chubby nine-year-old girl there were two terrible things about being immobile. I was, first of all, put on a strict diet. I cannot forget being denied a second bowl of spaghetti by my mother, who told me that if I got too fat I wouldn't fit in the cast. The cast became a tight chemise I could not take off, not even for a minute to let my hips run loose.

But more terrible yet than the diet was having to relieve myself in a bedpan. That meant that whenever I felt the urge I had to call for my mother. If my brother and my cousins were in the room playing, I had to announce to them to leave the room; otherwise, I wouldn't allow my mother to lift up the covers and slide the pan under me. Once, when she was busy entertaining friends in the living room, she didn't come fast enough and I had an "accident." I felt miserable knowing that everyone knew.

Perhaps because I was told that it was important to keep my body from bursting out of the cast, I became severely constipated. Or, maybe, being an invalid, my bowels seemed to be the only part of my body I could willfully control. My mother would bring in the bedpan and urge me to go, which was impossible so long as she stood waiting and watching. On one occasion, a week passed without my making a bowel movement. Keeping a secret has never been one of my mother's virtues. She spread the word to the entire family that Rutie was not making *caca*. Zayde, my maternal grandfather, whom I adored, appeared one day with a bottle of prune juice. When he poured out the juice it looked so dark and foul that it reminded me of excrement. My grandfather drank some to show me it was good, but when I tried to sip a little bit with a straw, I gagged and spit up into a tissue.

With his prune juice, my grandfather had tried to spare me the worse fate that my mother intended for me. Walking into the room with a determined look on her face, my mother meant to do something awful to get my bowels to obey. I pushed my mother away with all my strength, but with a quick turn of the ankle pole she had me flat on my stomach. Then she stuck in an enema. This was profoundly humiliating, profoundly violating, and my only comfort was to think of the excrement oozing into the bedpan as coming from someone else's body, not my own.

The public school sent a tutor to teach me and for a year I had private lessons in a wide range of subjects. My mother served us toasted English muffins at the start of the lesson and the tutor and I would work without interruption until midday. I came to enjoy those classroom sessions held around my bed as I enjoyed nothing else during my long convalescence. The days became bearable. It was wonderful to be the only student, to have a teacher all to myself, and I made tremendous progress in reading and math.

The accident took place just four years after we arrived in the United States as immigrants fleeing communist rule in Cuba. My father had brought into his exile a couple of pamphlets of Fidel Castro's speeches out of a bizarre sense of nostalgia, but we had no children's books or stories in English. Books were a luxury. The first goal was to acquire a television. The second goal, a used car. During my year at home, the tutor filled my bed with English storybooks and I read voraciously. When I returned to school I was no longer a Spanish-speaking child struggling with English, but among the more gifted kids who would be steered toward "special progress"—SP—classes in junior high school. The accident spurred my assimilation.

I also discovered, about a year after I returned to school, that I could no longer see the biggest letter on the eye chart. During my year in bed, in which I always faced the same direction, always looked out upon a world that was no bigger than the bedroom I shared with my brother, my field of vision shrank. My eyes, not needing to take in the wider world, contracted until I could only see what was closest to me, the little world of my bed and my immobile body lying there, squeezed tight into its corset.

While writing this essay, I asked my mother if, indeed, she never thought to change my position, so I wouldn't always be facing in the same direction. She immediately became defensive, even annoyed, about my question. How was I going to change your position? You think the room was that big? How was I going to take you outside, when the doctor said you should not be moved? There was an edge to her voice. I was making her feel guilty. I decided I would show her how grown up I was. I'm not accusing you, I said to her in an even voice, I'm just trying to remember. But I was lying. Of course I was accusing her.

Our first summer in the United States, in 1962, we lived with my grandparents, crammed into their apartment in Brooklyn. They were both working in a fabric store, my grandmother earning five dollars less than my grandfather. My grandfather—Zayde—knew the owner from the days when he bought lace from him for his store in Havana. He got a job for my father and by the end of the summer we moved to our own apartment in Briarwood, a neighborhood of faded red brick buildings in Queens.

My mother was told Briarwood was one of the better neighborhoods in Queens, even though it was on the outskirts of Jamaica, a black working-class neighborhood where the overhead train used to roar above stores and houses like an angry thunder-god. To my mother, the street in Briarwood that would now be her home seemed extremely ugly, but she figured she just didn't know what counted as pretty and what counted as ugly in America. My Aunt Silvia, my mother's older sister, was the one who knew. Not only was she already living in Briarwood, she had married an American, my Uncle Bill. They had met by chance just before the revolution, when he was visiting Cuba and seeking to date a nice Jewish girl. Bill knew New York like the back of his hand and he knew Briarwood was a step up from the Bronx. So, during our first years in America, the family reconstituted itself in one brick building at 141–65 85th Road. Silvia and Bill and my cousins Danny and Linda lived on the fourth floor, my grandparents lived on the third floor with my Uncle Micky, a teenager soon to be married, and my parents, my brother, and I lived on the sixth floor.

At the time of the accident we lived in a one-bedroom apartment. My parents slept on a sofa bed, a Castro Convertible, in the living room, and my brother and I shared the bedroom. The world became so reduced for me that I can only begin to imagine how the accident devastated my parents emotionally and economically. I know that my father worked two and three jobs, delivering rental cars and even fumigating apartments, to pay hospital bills and the costly trips to Brooklyn by ambulance for the X-rays that were periodically done of my leg.

It later seemed to me that my parents might have been able to request more compensation. But I suspect they were insecure about their status as "aliens" in the United States, not yet having attained the necessary residency period to apply for citizenship. They were just grateful, I think, that they were innocent.

I was immobile for close to a year. The body cast, changed once, stayed on for nine months. Then for one month I had a trimmer cast on my right leg alone, but I was still confined to my bed. When I was released from the cast, a visiting nurse taught me to use crutches, first two, then one. The left leg had emerged from the cast looking like a hairy monster, but it felt strong to me and, most important, it felt like *my* leg. Trusting my good leg, I mastered the crutches and could go anywhere on them.

But when I was told it was time to walk again with both feet planted on the ground, I simply refused to believe that my right leg could sustain me. It didn't feel like *my* leg; it hung there limp, thick as molasses, unbending and foreign. How was I supposed to tell it to walk? No, it would never work. Never! And so I took to my bed again, to the despair of everyone around me.

There are some things my mother said to me when I was a child that got branded into my soul as though they were hot iron. During the period when my fear of walking was at its peak, she flung some of these hot-iron words at me. I imagine that by that time, after cleaning out my bedpan for a year, she had endured about all she could. As my mother busied herself changing the sheets of my bed, she began to talk about how soon I would be *una mujercita* and going to parties and dances. The boys, she blurted out, were going to see that from the waist up I was a pretty girl, but, wow, were they going to be disappointed when they saw what I was like from the waist down. She then went on to say that at the rate I was going I would grow up to be just like Abuela, my father's mother, who was very fat and sat in her chair all day and seesawed when she walked—and what a shame, with her face so pretty. . . .

The first nurse quit and said I'd never walk. Then they sent another nurse. She told my parents to let her handle me. What I needed was to be treated mean and hard. If they kept on pitying me, I'd be an invalid for life.

It wasn't just that I feared I would fall flat on my face and break my leg again. There was something I found even more unsettling: I simply could not, for the life of me, remember how to walk. Every shred of memory of how people did it—how they stood, moved one foot forward, then another, and got somewhere—had been erased. I begged the "tough" nurse not to force me to walk. I told her I wasn't ready, to please understand how afraid I was, to please wait just a little longer. And maybe, as my great-uncle recently said to me, I did need a strong push to get me walking. But how I wish I had been urged to stand on my own two feet again with just a touch more gentleness, a touch more loving kindness.

After I relearned how to walk I had a heavy limp that gradually went away with a long routine of physical therapy. It was at the Continental Avenue bus stop, as we walked together to the physical therapist's office, that my mother announced that my Uncle Micky and Aunt Rebeca were expecting a baby. By then I was certain that the knowledge I had intuitively grasped before the accident was resoundingly true. And do you know how people have babies?, my mother asked me. Yes, I said, hoping she wouldn't ask me to explain it aloud. But she wanted to be sure I understood, and she started saying, "*La cosa del hombre y la cosa de la mujer . . .*" (The man's thing and the woman's thing . . .).

"Yes, I know, I know," I said. And we kept walking.

I kept a diary during sixth grade that ran for about eight months in 1968. All I remembered of the diary was that it locked with a little key and that my mother had managed to pry it open once and find the boy's picture I had stashed inside. Recently, I asked my mother to look for the diary and it turned up in a box in her attic. My mother reported that the diary was still locked, but that it had apparently been torn open at some point; it was sealed with thick black tape, and the key was lost. Should she open it?, she asked. No, I said.

The diary is bound in a red fake leather, the pages have gilded edges, and it is small. I hold it in my hands for a few moments before I tear it open. I wonder whether the eleven-year-old girl will have much to say about what happened to her two years before. I only find two entries that refer to the accident. On January 21, 1968, I write to "Cheryl," the name I have given to the diary: "Today we went to Manhattan and then to this place where older people meet where my grandparents gave me a little party in my honor because I am well now. I'll tell you about my car accident one of these days!" Then on February 1, I report: "Now that I have time I'll tell you about my terrible car accident on April 30, 1966 where I broke the femur bone on my leg. Everybody else had practically nothing. Morrie had stitches on his head and so did Pappy. BYE FOR NOW." Not another word of the accident in those pages. The only intimation that the healing process has been thorny is an entry from July 26: "Mommy, me and Morrie went to Manhattan. Going down the stairs [of the subway] I sprained my foot. It was terrible. I even cried in front of Pappy's secretaries. Now I feel terrible."

And yet, while the accident is notably absent from the day-to-day recording of events, the lack of self-assurance of the eleven-year-old girl is so stark that it becomes the major theme of the diary. On February 11, I write, "Today the Perkals came over. We had delicious Cuban sandwiches, tempting doughnuts, and what is called in Spanish 'panetela borracha,' a drunk cake. We played Monopoly and bingo. Morris got my guitar out of tune. Pappy always blames everything on me. I bet he doesn't like me." On February 22, I note, "Mommy doesn't like me so much. She thinks I'm so mean." Again, on March 18: "Pappy gets mad at everything now. I really don't know what's happening to this family. He wants me to be Miss Perfection and compares me with everybody. Boy, can't he take me the way I am?"

It soon becomes clear that the tension in the family—which I, at age eleven am interpreting personally as a withdrawal of affection from me—stems from my parents' plans to move out of Briarwood as soon as I finish sixth grade. On April 30, the anniversary of the accident, I write, "Mommy and Pappy are now American citizens," which suggests that their status in the United States is finally secure. At the same time, it seems clear that they are apprehensive about whether they have attained the means to relocate themselves more firmly within the white middle class. The May 17 entry notes: "There is a plan that we, the 5th and 6th graders, in September will have to go to IS–8 in South Jamaica." Our public school in Briarwood was primarily white, with black students being bused in from Jamaica. Now white children were going to be the ones bused into black schools. And my parents, aware that by age eleven I am already a menstruating *mujercita* about to start junior high school, begin to dream of moving to Forest Hills, where the influences will be "better," more white and more Jewish.

My mother explains that we need to move *porque se está echando a perder el barrio*, "because the neighborhood is getting bad" (literally, as in referring to overripe fruit, "beginning to rot"), code language for saying blacks are moving in. I wonder now: Where do my parents learn their racism? In Cuba, a black woman cared for me, shared a bed with me, took me out to lunch with her to eat Chinese food. But in the United States I grow up with a raceless image of Cuban culture, a bleached out version of the culture, listening to Beny Moré, Pérez Prado, and Celia Cruz, but not knowing they are black. That in the United States my parents, with their thick accents, become Latinos, and therefore suffer many of the same humiliations as other people "of color" (like getting bad service at restaurants and being stared at in elevators because they are speaking Spanish), somehow becomes irrelevant. We are determined to become white, at least as white as other Jews.

But the apartment hunting seems to have been very stressful. I note on May 5: "Hebrew school was okay. Mom and Pop went looking for apartments and left me and Morris at the movie the Double Man with Yul Brenner. It was great. Pappy was in a pretty bad mood." On May 28, I note, "About the apartment, Mommy and Pappy have been arguing about it. Now Pappy gets angry at anything. I don't know how he can be so mean." On May 29: "Mommy and Pappy are still angry. Pappy is really being mean to Mommy." And again on June 1: "Pappy was in a bad mood just because I didn't give him a kiss!" And then on July 1: "Well, here we are at our new apartment. Mommy looked so nervous. I hope she gets better quickly. I helped a lot with the cleaning."

The new apartment was much nicer than our old one in Briarwood. It had a huge picture window that looked out at the remains of the 1964 World's Fair in Flushing Meadow Park. My parents furnished it in the most modern style of the day, with lots of glass and chrome and mirrors. But I know that it was not quite the apartment my mother had longed for. She had her heart set on one of the bigger apartments that were like houses, with two floors, and three bedrooms upstairs. My father said they couldn't afford that kind of apartment; it was already going to break his back just to pay for the two-bedroom apartment.

In the new apartment I entered into my adolescence. There, the migraines began, but I didn't yet know my condition had a name. What I knew was that a few times a month a dark shadow fell over my life.

The body doesn't forget.

I learned to walk again, but that old fear never quite went away. It was years before I could run. It was years before I took possession of my legs. I would see people with a leg missing, or in a wheelchair, or hobbling along with one big-heeled shoe and one little-heeled shoe, and I would see myself in them. I would think: that's you, that's you, except you they forced to walk, you they pushed out of bed.

Not until after I had given birth to my own child did I begin to regain confidence in my legs. In my early thirties I began to exercise. I enrolled in an aerobics class. After a few years, I found, to my surprise, that I could move gracefully, that my legs worked just fine. Soon I was in the aerobics class with the most challenging teacher, the one who used a lot of difficult dance routines. I had gotten so good that I no longer hid in a corner in the back of the room, but staked out a spot for myself at the front of the class with the other accomplished women.

And then, in 1991, the day after I turned thirty-five, while I was at the front of the room doing an especially jumpy dance number, I turned my eyes to the mirror to catch a glance at my feet. That was all I did. The next minute, I felt dizzy, strangely out of it. I stopped immediately and in a daze went and sat down on the wicker chair with the tropical-print cushion, next to the table with all the magazines about how to achieve the right body. The odor of sweat struggling with deodorant filled my nostrils. I became so nervous I felt certain I would never be able to get home alone. I called David, and he and Gabriel came to pick me up.

After that, things went downhill. When I went back to aerobics a few days later, just lifting my arms brought on the feelings of dizziness and doom. I felt I had to get out quick—as though an alarm were going off inside me. I ran to the locker room and frantically pulled off my exercise clothes. Come on! Quicker! Everything was racing inside me. This time, I told myself, I would get home alone, no matter what it took. I got into the car and drove off. Faster! Faster! All the familiar streets spun around me. I refused to pay attention. Optical illusions. Just keep driving. Don't look. Keep your eyes straight ahead.

If only my heart hadn't started to tear like a sheet of paper, I wouldn't have had to stop. I might have made it. I slammed on the brakes just as I felt myself passing out.

I was only five blocks from my house. I wanted to scream, but I needed all my energy just to be able to breathe. "Someone save me!" I wanted to yell, but I couldn't get the words out.

A young man in a black leather jacket and tall boots was coming down his porch steps. I waved him over. "Could you drive me home?" I asked in a small voice. He gave me a funny look, but he got into the car. I had already moved over to the passenger seat. "Just turn and go straight five blocks," I said, letting my head fall into my hands. Maybe this man is a rapist, I thought, but I've got to get home somehow. He drove me to my house, the Wedgwood blue Victorian house filled with antiques and Mexican pottery bought with my own money, and he said it had been no problem and that he would walk the five blocks back.

In a matter of days my body shut down. I began to feel terribly, terribly tired and terribly, terribly agitated. I had no idea what was wrong with me. Neither did the doctor. But when I told him I planned to go to a big anthropology conference two days later, where I had three speaking engagements, he said he thought it would be much wiser for me to stay home and rest. Without my asking, he filled out a disability form. I'll go anyway, I thought; I can't be that sick. But when the day came, I could barely get out of bed. And that same day David and Gabriel were leaving for Texas. They planned to visit David's parents, frighteningly nice white, retired schoolteachers with heavy southern drawls, from whom I have studiously kept my distance to protect myself—as I see it—from being swallowed up by their Americanness. It had seemed like a perfect plan: I would spend a weekend at my anthropology conference in Chicago and they would spend a weekend in Dallas. We would go to the airport together, take separate planes, and then meet a few days later. Instead, I ended up staying home in my bed. I was fortunate that three women friends checked in on me during that hellish weekend when fear, deep and unspeakable, became my most constant companion.

At the time, I felt myself racing against the clock to finish my book *Translated Woman*, the life story of a Mexican street peddler. It was already late November and I had set a final deadline for myself to have the book completely done and in my editor's hands before I left on a two-week trip to Cuba at the end of December. The trip to Cuba had me extremely worried, and though I desperately wanted to go, another part of me wanted to just pull the covers up over my head and forget the whole idea. I would be traveling with David and leaving Gabriel behind with my parents, who had heightened the worry level by saying that I would be lucky if Fidel Castro let me return home. My parents even demanded that I write out a will and leave them custody papers for Gabriel. Nothing scared me more than the thought of never again seeing my son, who was almost five, the same age I was when we left Cuba.

Like other children taken into exile in the United States after the Cuban revolution, I had grown up internalizing the cold war between the United States and Cuba. I had absorbed both the Cuban immigrant paranoia about Cuba as a dangerous place, best left behind forever, and the United States ideology about Cuba as an enemy and a threat. There was also another issue for me, as a Cuban Jew. I kept asking myself what exactly I hoped to find in Cuba. After all, the members of my family were immigrants in Cuba, too. My grandparents, Jews from Byelorussia, Poland, and Turkey, had immigrated to Cuba in the 1920s, after the United States set sharp limits on Jewish immigration. All of my homelands, it seemed, were lost.

To calm these worries, I got into bed with my book manuscript, spreading the various versions of the text all around me. There in my bedroom on the second floor I decided that either I would finish the book or the book would finish me. Soon I discovered that I felt uncomfortable in any other part of the house. I took to bringing up a tray in the morning with water, rice, and ginger cookies, the only things I seemed to have an appetite for, which I nibbled on in the course of the day. I couldn't stand on my feet for long without getting dizzy, and I would return to my bed out of breath just from going up and down the stairs. I cursed myself for having wanted such a big old house with two floors—the very kind of house my parents had been unable to achieve when I was growing up. The only room I could bear to be in, my bedroom, was the smallest room in the house. I retreated to that room as though I were the littlest woman in a set of nested Russian dolls.

After David and Gabriel returned from Texas, I saw the doctor once more. This time, just sitting in the backseat as David drove to the clinic precipitated a flood of heart palpitations. As soon as I entered the clinic, my legs began to feel like Jell-O and I asked for a wheelchair. And this time, the doctor came up with a diagnosis: my body was physically depressed and I needed an antidepressant to snap out of it. The medication would cause drowsiness and blurry vision, he said, but it would help in the long run. Dizzy as I was, I asked a million questions. Isn't it silly to take a drug that will make me tired when I'm already tired? Won't I get better just with rest and a good diet? Do I really need a drug? Casting hard blue eyes on me, the doctor replied that he knew from clinical experience that people like me took years to recover without a drug.

He turned his back and began filling out more disability forms. I had told him I was planning a trip to the Caribbean the following month. I didn't tell him it was Cuba I planned to visit. He'd think I was a communist. And then who knows what he would prescribe? He said I would not be strong enough to undertake any travel for a long time.

I paid my bill and David wheeled me to the outer office. Gabriel, who had been hyperactive during my visit to the doctor, running up and down the hallways like a wild boy, refused to put on his coat. When David approached him, he would run away and laugh. Tired of having two children to care for, David suddenly fell apart, crying and scolding Gabriel at the same time. Soon Gabriel was crying and screaming at the top of his lungs. Everyone in the waiting room watched in horror. I sank into the wheelchair. Still crying, Gabriel finally wriggled into his coat and climbed on to my lap. David wheeled us both to the car. My legs hung down from my body like a marionette's legs. I had no strength left in them anymore.

During the weeks before I came to an understanding of what I was experiencing, I lived in a space of terror. A phone call to a psychiatric emergency number finally provided a ray of light: I had gotten caught in a spiral of anxiety and had developed agoraphobia as a result of confining myself to my bed. Once I understood my condition, I could begin to get well. I read various books on anxiety and learned how common panic attacks and agoraphobia are in women, especially contemporary women, who, as Carol Becker has written, "live in . . . a state of expectation, fearful about 'struggling for autonomy,' waiting anxiously for the ax to fall. . . . They expect to pay some price for the upheaval they have caused, yet are uncertain what the cost might be or what form of punishment they might be subjected to. Often the punishment is nothing more nor less than extreme, amorphous, and unrelenting anxiety. . . . Anxiety is an emotion of conflict—mind and body, internal and external reality, child self, adult self. . . . Anxiety will always accompany the unknown. It is an unwanted but unavoidable catalyst to change."[1]

Empowered by this knowledge, I finished my book. And I was able to push the terror back and go to Cuba, despite the doctor's advice and my parents' paranoia, and return, safe and sound and inspired. I dropped the doctor with the hard blue eyes, though not without writing a letter of complaint to the head of the clinic.

Exposure therapy, my self-help books claimed, was the best method for getting over panic attacks and the phobias they tend to set off. To conquer fear, return to the very sites that scare you, engage in the very things that chill you to the quick. For me, this meant going back to my aerobics class, where it all began.

At first, I was afraid to go alone, so David came with me. I found I could still do all the routines perfectly, but the room seemed to be spinning around me. I looked at myself in the mirror and felt a strange dissociation from the woman who was swinging her arms and legs about to the tune of the music. Exposure therapy, I kept saying to myself. Hang in there. I got through that class okay. Confident, a few days later I returned with David for another class.

Everything was going well and my inner voice was saying all the positive things it was supposed to say. You're doing fine, you're doing fine, you're not that nine-year-old girl anymore, your legs are healed, you can dance, you can do anything you want, you're doing beautifully. The room spun around me, but I kept moving. And then suddenly I had a sense of being in the ocean, and of being knocked down by the waves. They were pushing me down, deep into the water. I was nine again and crying, doing the aerobics and crying. I was seeing the darkness and the car flying over the divider. I was hearing the crash of broken glass and the moans of young men dying. And I was saying to my parents that I forgave them, that I wished they could have saved me, but I understood they had done what they could. Then I had to stop. The teacher told me to keep walking, not to sit, and I went off to the locker room, with David following, and paced back and forth, back and forth, until my heart settled itself. Then I cried and cried and cried for the nine-year-old girl who didn't get out all her tears and for the thirty-five-year-old woman who desperately needed her husband's shoulder because she had grown afraid of her own life.

It was unbelievable to me that I could have an intellectual understanding of my illness and still find it so difficult to physically carry out the tasks I set for myself. I was astonished at how difficult it was for me to get into a car again. I would become so breathless I had to roll down the car windows all the way in the height of winter to feel I had enough air. Weeks passed before I would get behind the wheel. Finally, I did it, and from then on I forced myself to be the one to drive to wherever David, Gabriel, and I needed to go. Driving by myself was a harder struggle, but that too would eventually become possible.

Through all this, I thought of my mother. For years and years after the car accident, she would clutch the sides of the car whenever my father slammed on the brakes or hit the accelerator to pass another car. He would become furious at her for her nervous reactions, saying they made it impossible for him to drive calmly. How sorry I felt for her at those times.

My mother's deepest desire, now that she and my father live on a tree-lined street in a neighborhood of small brick houses, is to get her driver's license and be able to drive. She has taken some driving lessons, but she can't quite muster the courage to get behind the wheel. Every time I see her, she tells me that this year she's going to drive. She's promised it to herself. *Sin falta*, she says, no matter what it takes, and she looks at me with the saddest eyes.

I had always known that one day I would tell the story of the car accident. And yet I kept censoring it, wanting to remain loyal to the adult injunction not to make too much of the whole thing, to insist that it could have been much worse. I would tell friends about the accident and my broken leg, and found that

I'd get irritated if they showed too much sympathy for the girl in the cast. I certainly had no sympathy for her. She had been a crybaby and a coward and I was ashamed of her. Not until my unconscious restaged, so many years later, the memory of my confinement to my bed and the dread of having to stand on my own two feet did I begin to feel empathy for the young girl I had been.

A fuller empathy came afterward, from the stories and inter-pretations I read to try to understand why the girl in the cast had resurfaced. If, as Alice Miller argues, coming to terms with one's childhood is a process of mourning, of "giving up the illusion of the 'happy' childhood," I needed to find others with whom to share my grief.[2]

One text that spoke to me immediately was an essay published in 1959 by the psychologist Marjorie Leonard, which explored the case of a two-and-a-half-year-old girl named Nancy, who had developed an intense fear of walking after recovering from a leg fracture caused by her fall from a kitchen counter. The cast stayed on Nancy's leg for only three weeks, but when it was removed she refused even to stand up and would cry bitterly if coaxed, urged, or scolded to try walking. Nancy's parents said she had been "a gay little girl before the accident," but afterward, "she appeared continuously unhappy, whined and cried."

Marjorie Leonard, working with Nancy as a Freudian psychoanalyst, came to the conclusion that the girl's fear stemmed from inner conflicts about her hostile feelings toward a younger brother who had just been born at the time of her accident. After play therapy, in which Nancy was able to act out her aggression on a set of dolls, including castrating the male doll, Nancy started to walk again, although cautiously and with a limp. As Marjorie Leonard astutely notes, "With the magical thinking common to children at that age, Nancy must have believed that her 'bad' impulses were perceived by her parents and that they had let the accident happen in order to punish her. . . . To resume walking meant being faced with the possibility of committing an aggressive act."[3]

No one thought to call in a psychoanalyst to figure out why I was afraid to walk. Such behavior was impossible for people of our class and immigrant status. But I can't help thinking that maybe at two and a half they would have taken pity on me and not pushed so hard to get me to walk before I was ready. The young girl, soon to become a *mujercita*, inspired only impatience.

Of course, I recognize that, in the end, I was lucky. Lucky because I healed well. Lucky because the doctor took not only my broken leg seriously but my future seriously.

I suspect things would have turned out differently had my skin not been white. Henry Louis Gates, Jr., the African-American literary critic, was not so lucky. At the age of fourteen, he incurred a hairline fracture of his leg while playing touch football. Unaware of the fracture, Gates continued to use the leg until the ball-and-socket joint of his hip finally tore. The white doctor who attended to him, in the Appalachia of 1964, mistakenly diagnosed his injury as a torn ligament in the knee and decided to put Gates in a walking cast. While plastering his leg, the doctor engaged the young Gates in a conversation about his future. Gates wanted to be a doctor when he grew up. So the white doctor thought he would throw him a couple of challenging questions. But Gates knew all the answers; he knew who discovered sterilization, who discovered penicillin, and who discovered DNA. Gates recalls that he thought his answers "might get me a pat on the head. Actually, they just confirmed the diagnosis he'd come to." And Gates goes on to describe how racism had everything to do with what happened to him and his leg:

"He stood me on my feet and insisted that I walk. When I tried, the joint ripped apart and I fell on the floor. It hurt like nothing I'd ever known.

"The doctor shook his head. 'Pauline,' he said to my mother, his voice kindly but amused, 'there's not a thing wrong with that child. The problem's psychosomatic. Your son's an overachiever.'"

Although Gates's mother immediately transferred her son to the University Medical Center, the damage had already been done. In years to come, Gates would limp through college while suffering from severe pain as the joint calcified, shortening his leg. Only at the age of forty, as a prominent man of letters, did he have hip-joint surgery to lengthen his leg. At last he was able to throw away his bricklike orthopedic shoes. But because a white doctor had presumed that "a colored kid who thought he could be a doctor was headed for a breakdown," Gates spent twenty-five years wondering how it feels to wear real shoes.[4]

Oliver Sacks's book *A Leg to Stand On*, an account of his recovery from severe damage to his leg during a solitary mountain climb in Norway, sat unread on my bookshelf for years. After re-encountering the girl in the cast during aerobics, I knew the moment was ripe to read Sacks. As I expected, the book shed light on my experience. Both as a patient himself, and as a doctor questioning other patients, Sacks learned that almost anyone who injured a limb, "and whose limb had then been casted, out of sight, out of action, had experienced at least some degree of alienation: I heard of hands and feet which felt 'queer,' 'wrong,' 'strange,' 'unreal,' 'uncanny,' 'detached,' and 'cut off'—and, again and again, the phrase 'like nothing on earth,'" Sacks writes eloquently of the difficulty of repossessing alienated limbs, especially in a medical context where healing is supposed to occur as soon as the injured limbs have mended. And yet healing calls for more than a physiological mending; it calls for a full restoration of one's sense of being in one's body and in the world. Immobilized and bedridden, the patient succumbs to "prisoner syndrome," in which visual space contracts, together with the whole of one's existence. Getting better involves not only the ability to use the injured limbs again but regaining the freedom to emerge "from self-absorption, sickness, patienthood, and confinement, to the spaciousness of health, of full being, of the real world." To stand confidently on one's own two feet, the posture of humanity for millennia, becomes for Sacks the symbol of full recovery: "The motions of uprightness, that physical-and-moral posture which means standing-up, standing-up-for-oneself, walking, and walking-away—walking away from one's physicians and parents, walking away from those upon whom one depended and hung, walking freely, and boldly, and adventurously, wherever one wishes."⁵

I cried reading these passages. And I really do mean cried. Like La Llorona, the Weeping Woman of Mexican lore, who is said to weep for the children she abandoned, I wept with fury, wanting to retrieve the child I once was and give her the understanding, the words, the knowledge, I now had. Reading about the terror Sacks experienced after only three weeks as a patient, I imagined the terror of being nine and immobile for almost an entire year. Here was Sacks, the neurologist, a man with credentials, bravado, an array of psychological, physiological, and perceptual concepts, and there was I, a child, disempowered, disembodied, lacking the language to clarify my pain.

But it wasn't just for the child that I cried; I wondered, too, about the grown-up woman reading Sacks. I wondered whether the world was as wide open and boundless for her as Sacks seemed to think it was for himself. It would never have occurred to me to go off alone to climb a 6,000-foot mountain in Norway without telling a soul about my whereabouts.[6] I would never want to be that alone in the world. And as a woman, I can't walk freely, boldly, and adventurously, wherever I wish. I just don't feel that safe.

The girl in the cast grows up to be a woman in a cast.

P erhaps women have forgotten girls," writes Carol Gilligan in an essay about her work fostering "healthy resistance and courage" in girls on the edge of adolescence. Her conversations with girls just beyond the sixth grade suggest to Gilligan that the threshold between girlhood and womanhood is a time when girls are pressured to become disconnected from their bodies, their anger, and their knowledge. "On a daily basis," Gilligan asserts, "girls receive lessons on what they can let out and what they must keep in, if they do not want to be spoken about by others as mad or bad or simply told they are wrong."[7] And so, at this age, girls lose confidence in themselves and begin to delegitimize their voices and perceptions. They fear that if they speak what they know they will be excluded from relationships, left unbearably alone. Under these circumstances, girls choose to not know what they know, beginning already the process of silencing the self that is so emblematic of women's depression.[8] For Gilligan, the only hope of breaking this cycle in women's development is for women to enter into relationships with girls, not as perfect role models who keep girls from feeling their sadness and their anger, but as women "harboring within themselves a girl who lives in her body, who is insistent on speaking, who intensely desires relationships and knowledge, and who, perhaps at the time of adolescence, went underground or was overwhelmed."[9]

Gilligan's desire to see the boundaries between girls and women dissolve stems from a feminist vision that can imagine how, one day, the underground knowledge women have stored inside themselves since girlhood will cease to be merely psychologically corrosive and become, instead, a public resistance that will remake the world. Certainly, this vision is utopian and not attuned enough to multiple paths of resistance.[10] But its redeeming quality is the challenge it poses to the girl/woman dichotomy, suggesting a need to overcome the classical self/other dichotomy that structures most autobiographies of childhood. If the woman is, in some ways, already harbored in the girl, and the girl in the woman, then Richard Coe's definition of "the childhood"—as a literary structure that is "complete exactly at the point at which the immature self of childhood is conscious of its transformation into the mature self of the adult who is the narrator of the earlier experiences"[11]—will need to be changed to make room for the more elusive border positionings of girls and women.

The House on Mango Street, a coming-of-age story by the Chicana writer Sandra Cisneros, is a model of how to construct a narrative that respects the fluidity of the border between the girl and the woman. The story exemplifies how the underground knowledge of girls can become the basis for a new social order. Yet Cisneros is always aware, unlike Gilligan, of how ethnicity and class intersect with what girls know. In *The House on Mango Street*, written in a genre between poetry and prose, thirteen-year-old Esperanza, growing up in Chicago, reflects on the possibilities open to her as a Chicana from the barrio. Esperanza is given the space to tell her own story, but in a form that challenges autobiographical isolation. Her story is embedded within the web of stories that emerge from the destinies being chosen by the various girls who live on Mango Street, each of them in various stages of becoming women.

Almost all the girls have bought into a romanticism learned from storybooks and movies, which makes them want to grow up fast and get married, in hopes that this will be their ticket out of the barrio, their path to freedom and autonomy, to owning their houses, pillowcases, and dinner plates. But the shared experience of all these girls is that they end up confined to their houses, where they become virtual prisoners, like Rafaela, who "gets locked indoors because her husband is afraid Rafaela will run away since she is too beautiful to look at." Only on Tuesday nights, when her husband plays dominoes, can Rafaela lean out the window and allow herself to dream of a freer life, drinking the coconut or papaya juice she has asked the younger kids to bring her and wishing "there were sweeter drinks, not bitter like an empty room."

Esperanza is helped in her decision to maintain the young girl's questioning of romanticism by the fact that she is "an ugly daughter . . . the one nobody comes for." She chooses to model herself on the kind of woman she's seen in the movies "with red red lips . . . who drives the men crazy and laughs them all away." She wants a power that is her own. And, so, as she crosses the threshold into womanhood, Esperanza begins to wage a "quiet war. Simple. Sure. I am one who leaves the table like a man,

without putting back the chair or picking up the plate." By starting to wage her quiet war against sexism before leaving her father's house, Esperanza can envision a house that will be totally
her own, with "nobody's garbage to pick up after." Hers will be
the power of the writer, the one who will tell the stories of the
girl-women of Mango Street.[12]

Sandra Cisneros told me that it was precisely when she finished writing the vignette entitled "Beautiful and Cruel" that
she stood up and said of her protagonist Esperanza, "This girl
is a feminist." As she explained, *The House on Mango Street* is
supposed to be told from a young girl's perspective, but it was
written by her when she was a woman in her mid-twenties. In
those years, as a counselor to Latina college students, Sandra
Cisneros heard the stories of other barrio women struggling
against poverty and sexism to get an education; and it was these
stories, meshed with recollections of her own girlhood, that became the basis of her book.

Esperanza's voice is a young girl's voice inflected with the
feminism and the politics of the woman Sandra Cisneros hoped
she would one day become. For, indeed, Esperanza is a touch
overly courageous and resistant for a girl her age. If one looks
at how Sandra Cisneros wrote about herself in her diary at age
thirteen, it is clear that she was not yet the Esperanza of her
fiction. Her entry for August 23, 1967, announces: "I've made
out some rules so when I get back to school: 1. I'll try to be more
friendly and not so shy. 2. I'll try not to be so timid and answer
more questions. 3. And I will try to be dressed prim and nice."[13]

So it seems clear to me now: the woman has to throw an an-
chor back to the girl she left behind, the girl who's just barely

treading water, the girl who is still worrying about why she's so shy and timid and not dressed nice enough.

The woman who forgets the girl she harbors inside herself runs the risk of meeting her again—as I did—in the lonely space of a house that is her own in name only.

As the Indian-English novelist Salman Rushdie has written, it is impossible for emigrants to recover the homelands they left behind. The best they can do is "to create fictions, not actual cities or villages, but invisible ones, imaginary homelands."[14] It seems to me that the notion of an imaginary homeland is very helpful for thinking about childhood. Aren't all of our childhoods imaginary homelands? Aren't they fictions about places left behind? Homelands from which we have become exiled in the process of growing up and becoming adults? In becoming adults we are encouraged to put the child behind us, to disbelieve our own stories and our own childhoods.

Here I assert that the body is a homeland—a place where knowledge, memory, and pain is stored by the child. Later, the woman that the child has become will search and search and search in her adult language for that child, but find that, like Hansel and Gretel trying to return home, the place markers have vanished. She finds that the path back leads to an imaginary homeland—that space on the frontier of consciousness where, as James Olney put it, words fail, but meanings still exist; where meanings—unspoken, inchoate, raw, and throbbing with life—wait to be found, to be given voice.[15] Inevitably, living a childhood and writing about it as an adult are fundamentally different experiences, but the value of autobiography is that it creates forms of embodied knowledge in which the (adult) self and the (child) other can rediscover and reaffirm their connectedness.[16]

The girl in the cast lives within the woman who won't move, can't move; the woman who has been stopped in her tracks, the woman who will not make up her mind as to how to place herself in relation to the lost homeland, the Cuba that is part memory, part forgetting, part longing. It is a homeland she doesn't know if she even has the right to claim as her own. It is a homeland so imaginary that she will only accept as evidence that it exists when her body forces her to stop, listen, and look.

F or several weeks after my return from Cuba, I have a distinct fear, when I set foot in the street, that I will not be able to find my way back to the Wedgwood blue Victorian house. I worry that a sudden oblivion will strike. The fear is so acute that I want to pin a piece of paper on my blouse with my address, just in case anybody finds me wandering around, lost.

Slowly the fear subsides. I calm down. I talk to myself in the supportive voice psychologists advise you to cultivate. I say, You went to Cuba and you came back. You see? It is possible. Don't be afraid anymore, little girl.

And during those weeks, when I seem to be driving in circles around Ann Arbor, I call to mind the teenagers who were returning from a discotheque dance at Murray the K's World in Roosevelt, Long Island, in 1966, when their car took off and flew, like a bird gone mad. And finally I stop hating them. Finally I mourn for them. Finally I pray that they are blessed among the dead.

CHAPTER 5

GOING TO CUBA

Writing Ethnography of
Diaspora, Return, and Despair

E ven now I am wavering. Even now I am crazily trying to find a way to undo all my plans. Tomorrow, I could get on a plane and attend the meeting of the American Ethnological Society in Austin, Texas, where, for the first time in the history of this society, border anthropologies and border anthropologists, Latinos and Latinas, will be at the top of the agenda. Tomorrow, I could, still, get on a plane and go to Cuba. It is 11:29, not yet noon in Ann Arbor. My heart beats frantically. I didn't know I'd be able to travel to Cuba until a week ago, when, late as always, a fax arrived informing me that my visa was approved—to be exact, what I get when I travel to Cuba is not a visa but a re-entry permit, because by Cuban law I'm still a Cuban national, who happens to reside abroad, "in the exterior." If I rush like mad, I could do it: get on the phone and call Cuba, as many times as necessary, so they'll send a fax to the travel agency in Havana telling them I have the visa, so the travel agency in Havana will then send a fax to the travel agency in Miami, so the travel agency in Miami can issue me the ticket to travel to Havana legally and not get fined ten thousand dollars by the United States government for violating the embargo against trading with the enemy. I could do it: run out and buy soap, detergent, paper, pens, books, and other gifts, quickly decide on the grades for my two courses, cancel my flight to Austin and buy a ticket to Miami, print out my paper, write the first thing that comes to mind for my discussant comments, give both these texts to one of my students to read for me, kiss Gabriel good night and promise him this will be the last trip in a long while, and call my mother, so she'll worry for me every day I'm gone and in that way ensure I return safely from the forbidden country. Since December I have known that there was a conflict with the dates of the AES meetings and the event in Cuba. At some point I knew I'd have to make a choice: Texas or Cuba, the acquired borderland or the abandoned homeland. I'd assumed, from the beginning, that if the visa arrived, I'd go to Cuba. It is 11:56. On April 25, 1995. Still early enough for me to change my plans.

I want desperately to go and attend the event to which I've been invited: a tenth-anniversary celebration for *Vigía*, an independent cultural arts magazine created by a talented and energetic group of poets and artists in the provincial city of Matanzas. *Vigía* draws on an aesthetic that is self-consciously about material scarcity; its creators use scraps of tissue paper, carton, and cardboard, and drawings and calligraphy done by hand to produce books that are mimeographed in editions of 200, each numbered and unique. The desire to make beautiful books, not just functional, mass-produced texts—at a moment when the merchandising of socialist Cuba is so rampant that even images of Fidel Castro and Che Guevara are on sale as tourist souvenirs—is not simply daring; it is an act of faith in the utter necessity of the cultural arts. Lately, *Vigía* has been reaching out to Cubans in the diaspora. In a recent issue of their magazine, *Vigía* published poems by Cuban-Americans and a Spanish translation of a chapter from my *Translated Woman*.

The tenth-anniversary celebration of *Vigía* was to have been a major international event with participation of many friends and supporters abroad as well as writers and artists from Cuba. *Vigía* had hoped to put up all the foreign guests in a hotel and provide meals and transportation. However, when they put in requests to the UNEAC (National Union of Writers and Artists of Cuba) and the Ministry of Culture for visas for the foreign guests—which included Mexicans and Spaniards as well as myself and three other Cuban-Americans—they were turned down. The officials claimed that *Vigía* had not followed correct bureaucratic procedures. But the major error was that *Vigía* had dared to plan an international cultural event without obtaining permission first from official authorities. The Ministry of Culture refused to authorize visas for the foreign guests, or pay for their hotel and expenses; any foreigners who attended the event would have to do so as tourists, not as participants and guests of the Cuban government.

I had been writing letters constantly throughout the previous months to the president of the UNEAC telling him of my interest in attending the *Vigía* event and of my hope that he would authorize my visa. But I'd gotten no reply. The day after I bought plane tickets for myself, David, and Gabriel to travel to Austin the fax arrived from him, informing me that the *Vigía* festival had been canceled, or rather, postponed, as he put it, until the Havana Book Fair the following February. However, he added that if I needed to go to Cuba during those same dates to do research, he would authorize my visa.

I immediately phoned the editor of *Vigía* in Matanzas and learned that, in fact, the festival would still take place, but without the support of the government. They would do things as they had always done at *Vigía*, put people up in each other's houses, make do with resources they would all pool together. "Light a candle for us tomorrow," I heard him say. "At 8:30 in the evening. But I still hope you'll be here to light it with us." Listening to him speak so humbly, with such idealism and hope, I felt I had to do everything in my power to get to Cuba, if only to demonstrate my solidarity with *Vigía* and protest the Cuban government's effort to shut down their event.

For their tenth-anniversary festival, the members of *Vigía* had worked around the clock to produce ten new books and a new edition of their magazine, which included writings by several Cuban-Americans, among them two of my poems. Only in Matanzas, the "Athens of Cuba," was I being reborn, in this lifetime, as a poet. That, I knew, was another reason I had to get to Cuba: to claim that identity, to be the poet in my native country that I'd not been able to be in my adopted country. But how, with time so short, and all the bureaucratic details still to be worked out, would I get to Cuba? Unable to accept the geographies of time and space, I again struggled to be in two places at the same time, just as I had struggled between going to Spain and staying in Miami Beach when my grandfather was dying.

After hanging up I called my friend Nena in Chicago. Nena is Cuban like me, also came to this country as a child, also grew up to become a professor. She's a veteran of the second-generation Cuban-American search for connection to Cuba. She's traveled to the island dozens of times, used to be a member of the Antonio Maceo Brigade, which mobilized a generation of young Cuban-Americans who wanted to believe in the Cuban revolution, children of exiles who challenged their parents, begging the fatherland to repatriate them (but Fidel Castro didn't choose to take back these radical children who wanted to reclaim the revolutionary inheritance their bourgeois parents had refused to transmit to them; Papá Fidel told the *maceítos* they could do more good for the revolution abroad). I had been sharing my doubts and indecision with Nena for an entire week, and she'd been listening patiently. "Cuba is an addiction," she said. And she's trying to get over it.

I know Nena is right. After my initial spell of fear and paranoia about returning, I've gone back several times. Once you've returned and seen and photographed the places where your family lived, the places where you left behind your childhood, once you've returned and seen that the island's heart still pumps blood, without you, what is left to go back for? We invent research projects for ourselves, but ultimately we go back to prove to ourselves we're not afraid to go back.

Nena too was supposed to have attended the *Vigía* event, but lately she's been making public her criticism of the Cuban government, and so she didn't get the same personal visa offer I got from the president of the UNEAC. I tell her how important it seems to me to go and show my solidarity with *Vigía*. Gently, she tells me: "Look, Ruth, that's the Joan of Arc position so many women have taken, thinking they'll be able to make a difference, thinking they will be the ones who will be able to save Cuba. But the real changes will have to come from inside. And you know something? Cuba will always be there." Of this last fact she's trying to convince herself, too. The problem, we both recognize, is that, ironically, it's incredibly difficult to get into Cuba if you're Cuban-born. Only a handful of us among the so-called worms of the revolution are considered trustworthy enough to be let in. So we're accustomed to jumping at the chance to run to Cuba whenever the government deigns to permit our "re-entry." The visa always arrives late, when it arrives at all, but we're ready to drop everything and go to the island at the drop of a hat.

"You know," Nena says to me, speaking now as the mother of two daughters, "your son will only be eight years old once, but Cuba will always be there. Even *Vigía* will still be there." That's one of the stories I'm not telling: the story of the professional working mother and her conflicts about leaving her son behind, yet again, for another extended absence. I've been traveling almost every weekend for the last two months, giving lectures at different universities. I'm just back in Ann Arbor from a stint in Iowa. The trips are beginning to put a strain on our little nuclear family. David says Gabriel is sad when I'm away, that he worries about me.

In the case of Cuba, all this is complicated by the fact that return trips—for me and all second-generation Cuban-Americans—are always about recovering our abandoned childhoods. My family left Cuba when I was almost five, and I return to Cuba in search of memories I never find. As Carmelita Tropicana puts it in "Milk of Amnesia," her comic performance piece: "I am like a tourist in my own country. Everything is new. I walk everywhere hoping I will recall something. Anything. I have this urge to recognize and be recognized. To fling my arms around one of those ceiba trees and say I remember you. . . . I want a crack in the sidewalk to open up and say, yes, I saw you when you jumped over in your patent leather shoes holding onto your grandfather's index finger. But it doesn't happen. There is no recognition from either the tree or the sidewalk."[1]

Although the recognition doesn't happen, in Cuba I reconnect with the family of the black woman, Caro, who cared for my brother and me until the day we left. It is through Caro's stories and memories that I recover the child my own family doesn't remember, the child who lost a country before she knew what it meant to even have a country. But I begin to wonder: Am

I recovering my childhood at the cost of being absent from my own son's childhood?

It is 3:48. The Marazúl travel agency in Miami should be open for at least another hour. But there's one more story, the one I really don't want to tell: what Texas represents for me. David is from Texas. Going to Texas I will have to see his brothers and his parents and confront what I have not wanted to confront: the distance I've traveled since we left Cuba, the distance I'm trying so hard to obliterate in my recent trips back and forth to the island, the distance between my diasporic Jewish Cuban identity and the ties that now bind me to a white Methodist Texan family. Like a tree in a storm, I furiously grip the soil on which I find myself, the soil of the country that adopted and adapted me. It is Texas that terrifies me now, much more than Cuba.

It is 4:02. I'm tired of struggling. I have the ticket, so I'm going to Austin—the borderland, not the homeland. Off again to be a truant schoolgirl, because I can't figure out, for the life of me, how to be a poet here.

Going or not going somewhere—Is that the essence of freedom? Or a consolation prize for those who don't have roots anywhere, anymore? During the months I wait, uncertainly, for my Cuban visa to arrive, I come to feel, deeply, the enormous sorrow of being countryless, the enormous rage of being countryless. And I also experience the other side of this: the enormous sorrow of having too much country, the enormous rage of having nothing but *patria*, nothing but fatherland—or death, *patria o muerte*, the nationalist Cuban credo. I think about my friends in Cuba who can't leave the island, not even to catch a glimpse of the countries that lie beyond the ocean spilling over the Malecón seawall. And I think about the Cuban-Americans I know who can't return to the island, not even to catch a glimpse of that ocean. Some of them were once welcomed on the island as "friends of Cuba," but the door shut in their faces when they became too critical of the regime. I worry for Nena. Will the door soon shut for her? One day—perhaps because I am saying this—will the door to Cuba finally shut for me?

All this going back and forth to Cuba makes me think that I ought to do something with my anguish and ambivalence besides write poems. Schoolgirlish despite myself, I want academic credit and brownie points. Maybe, I think, I should teach a course on Cuban culture. But I've hardly begun to imagine what in the world I will be able to tell students about Cuba in the throes of a Michigan winter when I find myself stuck; I can't think of a title to give my course.

Initially, it occurs to me to call it "Cuba Since the Revolution." But I realize that is only half of what I want to teach. What I want is a course that will consider contemporary Cuban culture as created by both revolutionary Cuba and the Cuban community in the United States. Cuban culture needs to be seen dialectically, questioning, rather than as reinforcing the usual border between Latin America (as everything that is the civilizational "other" of the United States) and Latins in America (that is, the people of Latin American heritage, lately totaling about thirty million, who live in these United States). Cuban culture, I feel, can best be understood as the product of an intellectual and historical relationship between those who stayed in Cuba and those who left Cuba after the revolution. For it is the relationship between the nation-state and its "others" that has become the central tragic Cuban counterpoint since Fidel Castro dared history not to absolve him.

In reflecting on what name to give this counterpoint, I play with the idea of calling the course "Cuba and Its Exiles." But that title raises a number of thorny questions: Can the one million Cubans in the United States still be considered exiles? Are they truly so different from other displaced people who have remade their lives here? Haven't they, or at least their children, after thirty-seven years of Castroism and less hope than ever of a permanent return to Cuba, finally become immigrants? Even Latinos? Even, as David Rieff would have it, simply Americans?[2]

Yet I can't quite bring myself to call the course "Cuba and Its Immigrants," either. On the other hand, while I reject the political agenda of the extremists in the exile community, I have come to respect the choice my parents and their generation made to leave, especially as I watch increasing numbers of intellectuals and artists of *my* generation, people I met in Cuba and expected to keep seeing *in Cuba*, also choose to leave and cross over to this side. But, of course, it's not leaving that puts the term "immigrant" at issue; it is return, the obstacles to return. Indeed, as long as leaving means a one-way ticket, as long as being able to travel freely to and from Cuba continues to be impossible, as long as leaving remains the only way of voicing dissent against the political, economic, and ideological crisis in Cuba, I think we have no choice but to admit that Cubans outside Cuba do live in a kind of exile, a state of existential limbo, a continual waiting for Godot. And, though often forgotten, so too do those Cubans living inside Cuba, their *insilio* mirroring our *exilio*.

In the midst of these ruminations, I come to the word "diaspora" and decide, finally, to call the course "Cuba and Its

Diaspora." By choosing diaspora I opt for undecidability, a refusal to submit to the tyranny of categories: Cubans outside Cuba are perhaps immigrants, perhaps exiles, perhaps both, perhaps neither, and Cubans inside Cuba are in certain ways perhaps more exiled in their *insile* than the so-called exiles themselves. Diaspora embraces all these possibilities and others, including earlier periods of displacement in Cuban history, and the complex legacy of nineteenth-century independence leader José Martí, who as both a Latino and a Latin American forged a dialectic of diaspora and return, which each of our Cubas claims in hopelessly one-sided ways. Diaspora also counters the Cuban tendency toward exceptionalism and the arrogance of insularity, allowing us to place the Cuban counterpoint within a wider framework of twentieth-century unbound nations, borderizations, and deterritorializations.[3]

Reading about new perspectives on Jewish and African diasporas, I arrive at a keener sense of how to frame my Cuba course. The engagement with the Jewish Diaspora is present in everyday Cuban life and sensibility outside Cuba. "Next year in Havana," which obviously mimes the Jewish Passover refrain, "Next year in Jerusalem," is a common toast among Cubans in Miami. Indeed, David Rieff claims that Miami Cubans have derived many of their behavioral and political styles from American Jews. The Cuban idea of *exilio*, after all, stems from Cubans living in close proximity to Jews in Miami Beach, who remain linked to another country, Israel, and who are still troubled about their own sense of difference and the threat of assimilation. As one woman in David Rieff's book remarked, "Just like the Jews, what is important to us is that we keep on saying it [Next year in Havana]. . . . That's what unites us, that feeling. It's an emotional thing, something no one should try to take away." And as the dream of return is postponed to an ever more indefinite future, the metaphor of the Jewish Diaspora seems yet more apt. After making the toast "Next year in Havana," a middle-aged man marked the passage of time by saying, "The first time I made that toast, I was still drinking milk with my dinner."[4]

Among the most compelling writing on the idea of the Jewish Diaspora is an essay by Daniel and Jonathan Boyarin that argues that Zionist positions, born of nineteenth-century European nationalism, contradict, and even defy, the biblical story, which "is not one of autochthony but one of always already coming from somewhere else." Judaism, they suggest, "as lived for two thousand years, begins with a people forever unconnected with a particular land, a people that calls into question the idea that a people must have a land in order to be a people. . . . Abraham had to leave his own land to go to the Promised Land; the father of Jewry was deterritorialized." Diaspora, they conclude, may well be Judaism's most important contribution to the world, showing "that peoples and lands are not naturally and organically connected . . . [that] a people [can] maintain its distinctive culture, its difference, without controlling land."[5] With humor rather than pathos, Philip Roth makes much the same point in his novel *Operation Shylock*, which tries to imagine a world where Jews must return to all the diasporan locations they once inhabited, for "the Diaspora is the normal condition and Zionism is the abnormality . . . the only Jews who *are* Jews are the Jews of the Diaspora."[6]

At issue here is a critique of the state of Israel as the culmination of Jewish history, as the ultimate homecoming and, therefore, end of Diaspora; a critique of the Israeli state as the embodiment of the Jewish nation, "among Jews who are increasingly ambivalent and puzzled by the uses and abuses of Israeli power."[7] One can readily see the analogy to Cuba: the Cuban diaspora likewise makes a distinction between the wandering nation of Cuba and the revolutionary state headed by Fidel Castro, in which history both begins and ends.

The literature on the African diaspora which has come out of black British critical writing offers another important perspective from which to rethink the Cuban diaspora. Paul Gilroy's focus on "roots" and "routes" in *The Black Atlantic* suggests that dwelling-in-diaspora has always been embedded in the way African-descended people have imagined the meaning of homeland.[8] Similarly, Stuart Hall, in a fascinating essay on cinematic representation, attempts to rethink the "positionings and re-positionings of Caribbean cultural identities" in relation to the African presence. Although Africa was "alive and well in the diaspora" when he was a child growing up in Kingston, Hall notes that people didn't refer to themselves or to others as having been at some time in the past "African." It was only in the 1970s, with the civil rights struggles, the postcolonial revolution, and the music of reggae, that this Afro-Caribbean identity "became historically available to the great majority of Jamaican people, at home and abroad." This "new Africa" became a privileged signifier of changed conceptions of Caribbean identity. At the same time, he reminds us, "Whether it is, in this sense, an *origin* of our identities, unchanged by four hundred years of displacement, dismemberment, transportation, to which we could in any final or literal sense, return, is more open to doubt. The original 'Africa' is no longer there. It too has been transformed. . . . Africa must at last be reckoned with . . . but it cannot in any simple sense be merely recovered. . . . We can't literally go home again." Hall suggests that the return to Africa must happen "by another route," that is, "what Africa has *become* in the New World, what we have made of 'Africa'—as we re-tell it through politics, memory and desire."[9]

I am drawn to these visions of diaspora as a site for the rec-reation of identity and for liberation from the credo of father-land or death. Yet I feel more hesitant about their bottom line, which is an unwillingness to believe in the possibility of return. Return, however, to what? Or where? If there is no true place of origin, no native land, only diasporas layered on top of diaspo-ras, what can return mean? To look back, as we know from the biblical story of Lot's wife, is to risk turning into a pillar of salt.

Really, it is better not to return, not to look back. Memory is sweeter. It is a *panetela borracha*, a cake drunk on sugar and rum. Cubans of the diaspora, who drink their sugarcane memories, their *guarapo*, on Calle Ocho and say they will not go back to Cuba until things there really change, must sleep more bliss-fully than those of us who can't keep from looking back. To look back, I tell you, is to look into the eye of power, to feel the salt burn. Some of us just don't learn.

The obsession with returning to Cuba that we find among second-generation Cuban-Americans has everything to do with the way the abandoned island became for us a forbid-den territory. By imposing a blockade against Cuba, the United States effectively cut off communication, and made the desire for a bridge especially urgent.[10] Lately, as I try to understand the Cuban relationship of "roots" to "routes," I am trying to see if there are connections to other Latino diasporas and com-munities. How, for example, does the second-generation search for Cuba compare and contrast with the search for Aztlán, a

legendary site of origin for the Aztecs, which came to be iden-
tified with the U.S.-conquered Southwest during the height of
the Chicano movement?[11]

I know that I came to my sense of Cuban-American identity
through my reading of Chicana/Chicano imaginings of home
and homelands. Experiencing in my own flesh the visceral reality of the U.S.-Mexico border, which I crossed so many times
bringing back Esperanza's story for *Translated Woman*, made
me think about the kinds of walls, and possible bridges, that
existed between Cubans of the island and the diaspora. At the
same time, I wondered about my privilege, as the bearer of a
U.S. passport, to cross borders. As an "exile" from Cuba, I had
benefited from unique U.S. immigration policies that gave me
symbolic capital as a defector from Fidel Castro's revolutionary
government. There was no such welcome mat for Mexican un-
documented immigrants, and Esperanza and other people who
accepted me into their intimacy never let me forget that I was
in Mexico as a *gringa* with *gringa* privileges and *gringa* money.

To think about these connections, which are fraught with
pain and anger and misunderstanding, we need as displaced intellectuals to begin an intercultural discussion of Latina/Latino
narratives of return to Latin American, Caribbean, and colo-
nized U.S. homelands. Although there is increasing interest in
transnational circuits, immigration and diaspora studies usually
focus on one-way journeys toward the United States. But Latino
diasporas also have an impact on the countries left behind, even
when, perhaps especially when, as in the case of Cuba, those
who leave are branded as unpatriotic, as traitors to the nation.

Those Latino/Latina narratives of return that do exist are
deeply ambivalent. Consider the beginning of Richard Rodriguez's memoir, *Days of Obligation*, in which he describes himself

on his knees, his mouth over the mouth of the toilet, vomiting up bits and pieces of Mexico and badly pronounced Spanish words. He's gone back to Mexico with the BBC to serve as a TV presenter for a documentary on the U.S. and Mexico. What irony there is in this, Rodriguez exclaims, he, "a man who has spent so many years with his back turned to Mexico." Rodriguez doesn't even bother to search for the village his father came from; he's content to find a televisable substitute, where he can *imagine* his "father as a boy, dreaming of running away."[12]

In *Getting Home Alive*, Rosario Morales expresses similar doubts: "*Home*, like Australians talking about an England they have never seen," she writes of Puerto Rico. Unlike Rodriguez, she returns to her father's real native village, but nevertheless concludes, "This is not home. Eleven years couldn't make it home. I'll always be clumsy with the language, always resentful of the efforts to remake me, to do what my parents couldn't manage. . . . I was shaped on Manhattan Island. . . . Ironic. On the plane down I'm conscious only of my soft tropical core. Here I'm only aware of the North American scaffolding surrounding it, holding it up."[13]

The ambivalence in these accounts is echoed among second-generation Cuban-Americans who have returned to Cuba.[14] We have gone to Cuba with our hearts in our hands and been received, by our family and friends, with their hearts in their hands. But more often than we dare admit, we have been met with suspicion, distrust, and security officials posing as colleagues and friends. Many no longer want to return. Others don't even think of the island of Cuba, when they think of islands at all. If they long for an island and can pay the price, they go to Belize or the Bahamas. If not, there is always plenty of *guarapo* on Calle Ocho. A few of us, though, are addicted to the island we love to visit, even though we know, deep down, we can't live there anymore. Still, we just aren't ready yet to let Cuba go. To let Cuba go is to let go of Cuba's dreams—huge, immense, gigantic dreams, in which we have wanted, desperately, to take part.[15] Our reluctant awakening—amid the leaky rafts of the *balseros*, the prostitutes of the Malecón, and the crumbling buildings of Old Havana—has been fitful, painful, and unspeakably sad.

After my initial frustration in trying to secure a visa to visit Cuba in 1992, I haven't had any more problems, and so far have been able to travel to the island easily and frequently— even though I am always kept waiting until the last minute for permission to travel. After working so hard to win the trust of the officials in Cuba, I worry about what it means that I'm getting the red-carpet treatment. Have I perhaps become too "pc"? Not "politically correct," but in the Cuban translation, *persona confiable*, a person who can be trusted not to air socialist dirty laundry in front of those who can use it against Cuba. Have I set myself up to be manipulated? Certain doors, I have noticed, are open for me that aren't open for some of the writers and artists who have become my friends in Cuba.

The fear that I'd been colluding with power in my trips to Cuba reached a crescendo in April of 1994, when I attended the state-sponsored dialogue strategically titled *La Nación y la Emigración* (The Nation and Its Emigrants) in order to indicate that the Cuban government doesn't recognize *the exile*. The aim of this dialogue, the successor to the famous 1978 *Diálogo* that led to the release of political prisoners and the family reunification program, was obstensibly to discuss the normalization of travel, business, and cultural exchange between the two Cubas. The

1978 dialogue had been with Fidel; the 1994 dialogue involved four top Cuban leaders and 219 "safe" diaspora participants, handpicked by the Cuban government. Although Fidel was absent, it was rumored he was watching the proceedings on video from the Palace of the Revolution.

It was then I came fearfully close to the dangerous seductions of power: in the privilege of being invited to return to help maintain the socialist revolution because I'd succeeded in the capitalist academic market; in the extravagantly plentiful buffet lunches and dinners, offering a variety of foods and drinks not available to ordinary Cubans; in the free four-star hotel room that overlooked the ocean; in the ease with which I could interact with top Cuban officials; in the invitation, as the dialogue drew to a close, to attend a reception with *El Comandante* (from which, out of respect for my parents, I stayed away). I was only able to relax when, after it was all over, one of my poet-friends in Cuba joked, "Hey, how come they never hold a dialogue with us?"

As I write, I am hearing the voice of a distinguished historian of Cuba in my ears. During a late-night drink at a conference in New Hampshire about "Cuba at the Crossroads," he left me and other companions speechless as he lashed out at those of us who had spoken critically of the current situation in Cuba. "I don't know why I still participate in these things. I don't know who we're speaking to anymore," he said, shaking his head. "I say, if you're going to speak against Cuba, then go do it there, tell it to them in Cuba, take a risk and see if they'll let you back in afterward. But don't do it here, where you just give grist to the mills of Mas Canosa [the right-wing Miami Cuban exile leader] and Jesse Helms." It was hard to listen to these words, so thick with anger and the righteous sense of which truths ought to be spoken in which places, words so reminiscent of those arguments among Jews about whether anyone in the Diaspora has the right to criticize Israel. This historian, whom I greatly respect, refuses to write Cuban history after 1959. He writes about everything that led to Cuba's revolution: Cuba's long struggle for independence, Cuba's justified quest to free itself from the yoke of U.S. domination, and that extraordinary moment when *pueblo* (people), *patria* (fatherland), and *patriarca* (patriarch) were fused as 1959 dawned. Refusing to speak of everything that has happened since 1959 is this historian's way of not betraying Cuba, not betraying what the dream of the Cuban revolution meant for the best hopes of Latinos and Latin Americans. More sadly, I hear him saying, "As a Latino kid growing up in the Bronx, feeling like we didn't count for anything, feeling like we were worse than shit, it meant something to me that Fidel could tell the gringos to go to hell. That meant something. I can't forget that." These words haunt me. German exile Bertolt Brecht wrote, "Pity the nation that needs heroes."

I am in Havana to distribute copies of *Bridges to Cuba*, an anthology of writings and art by second-generation Cubans of the island and diaspora. I speak about the project not only at the UNEAC but also at the rooftop meeting place of the Casa del Poeta (House of the Poet), which is also the home of poet Reina María Rodríguez. She herself is just back from a bridges-type encounter in Stockholm that included Cuban writers from both shores and is confessing that she went largely to bring home dollars to buy milk for her young daughter.

On Reina's rooftop, I try to explain to the group of young male writers gathered there what it was like for Cuban-Americans of my generation to grow up in the United States feeling that we had lost a country and needed to build a bridge back to Cuba. When I am done, one of the young men, a poet, turns to me and says earnestly that he, too, though he never left Cuba, feels he has lost a country, feels that Cuba, with its increasing tourism, prostitution, and ever more desperate search for dollars no longer belongs to him, either.

I am profoundly moved by the words of this young man and promise to meet with him again as well as with others who want to show me their work. My friend the Afro-Cuban poet Victor Fowler Calzada had warned me that with the publication of *Bridges to Cuba* I would now occupy the role of *promotora cultural* and would be viewed, not only as a clearinghouse for Cuban writing and art, but as a source for invitations to travel to the United States. He'd already told me there were friends of his who had stopped speaking to him because they envied the fact that he'd been able to travel to the United States. Now that he'd returned from his second trip, invited by me to attend a University of Michigan conference marking the publication of *Bridges to Cuba*, he had lost more friends, because he hadn't brought back, as they put it, anything concrete. Something concrete was a couple of invitations to travel to the United States.

So I shouldn't be surprised when I meet with the earnest poet and his three friends shortly before my presentation to the UNEAC and discover that they hope I'll be their personal bridge to the United States. Will I publish their work? Promote it? Let them know about any conferences they might attend? I want to encourage them yet not create false hopes. I only have a few minutes and find myself needing to cut them short. The more I struggle to let go, the more they struggle to keep me there. I have a sudden sensation of being lost at sea and of trying to reach the shore with each of them pulling at my arms and legs. I am the raft, the bridge, the piece of driftwood heading north. Yes, we've both lost our country, they and I, but with dollars in my purse, I can come and go.

Yes, I can come and go. Every now and then I worry that I am testing my luck too much. I wonder: Am I setting myself up to be in Cuba for the final horror, for the apocalypse? But seven months later, on a balmy July night, when the stars gleam like rhinestones, I am back, this time in an outdoor courtyard in Matanzas, belatedly reunited with my friends at *Vigía*, reading my poems in my own Spanish translations to a small audience of local poets, translators, editors, teachers, and artists.

On that night when the stars gleam like rhinestones, I am warned that there is someone from state security in the audience. The local communist party officials, I am told, brought in the editor of *Vigía* for questioning when they learned that *Vigía* had produced a small book of my poems and heard I'd be reading those poems in a public venue. They told the editor to remember that national security was involved. How could he casually invite a Cuban-American to give a presentation without consulting with them first? Didn't he know that Cuban-Americans, by definition, were suspect? Had he forgotten about the exile terrorist plots to bring down the revolution?

But I try not to worry, or think about my mother worrying, as I read my poems, which follow my ambivalent journeys back and forth from Cuba to the United States. No sooner am I done speaking than the young, pale-haired, strong-chested man in the faded yellow *guayabera* raises his hand to ask me a question. One of my friends meets my gaze and pretends to be dusting off imaginary dandruff from his shoulder, the pantomime commonly used to let you know someone is a *seguroso*.

I wait at the edge of my chair to hear what he will say. But I am so taken aback by what he asks that, at first, I can barely believe I've heard him correctly. What is my expert opinion, he wants to know, of the Cuban physique? Are Cubans the same as other people with regard to physique?

After a long and awkward pause it dawns on me that all the man knows about me is that I'm an anthropologist and so he has assumed that what I do is study human physical types. I fantasize saying to him, "My dear sir, in my expert opinion I have found Cubans to be the most beautiful and utterly perfect beings on earth, like no other humans. . . ."

In Matanzas I spend long hours talking to the book illustrator and artist Rolando Estévez about our different losses as members of the Cuban second generation. His compassion for those of us diaspora Cubans who feel we left behind our childhoods in Cuba stems from a quite different, and more devastating, experience of loss and mourning. He never left Cuba; it was his family who left him. His parents and younger sister emigrated to Miami when he was fifteen. By Cuban law, Estévez could not leave because he was of military age. His parents, of the white middle class, wanted desperately to leave. Forced to make a terrible decision—like so many other Cuban families—whether to sacrifice both children or save one at least, they left, planning to get Estévez out later. But when Estévez's parents were finally able to get him out of Cuba, Estévez refused to go. He couldn't forgive them for having left him behind. In the early 1980s, during the family reunification program, his parents returned to visit, but these trips took a toll on their health. After one of her trips, his mother fell into a coma, and when she awakened six months later she forgot she'd ever left a son behind in Cuba. When her memory came back, she remembered that her son, the artist, had refused to paint her a picture of a bird of paradise. He'd told her he was sorry but he only painted in black and white. His father developed a heart condition. He can eat anything he wants, the doctor says; it doesn't matter anymore. He is dying—and Estévez cannot get to Miami because United States immigration officials in Cuba won't give him a visa because they are sure he would defect.

Thirty years pass before Estévez and his sister see each other again. One year they even stand on opposite sides of the Berlin Wall. But finally, in Mexico, in 1994, while Estévez is there for a book fair, the brother who was sacrificed and the sister who was saved get to look each other in the eye. Even as the grown-up woman stands before him, Estévez still sees the eight-year-old girl with the two long braids that reach to her waist. He still sees the eight-year-old girl saying good-bye, clutching in her small hands the doll he'd gotten for her by standing all night outside a government store to be the first in line in the morning.

I visit their mother and father in their subsidized federal housing apartment in Miami. "You see how poor we are," the mother says. "Everything, everything we had, was for Cuba. To send to Cuba. That's why we never had anything for ourselves." As I am leaving, she remembers about the doll in the front closet. "Look," she says, pulling it out. And I look. I see a doll whose eyes have never shut.

While Victor Fowler was in Michigan he stayed at my house and we would talk late into the night. I asked him so many naive questions about Cuban popular culture and language that he came to call our conversations *Curso introductorio para cubanos tardíos* (An Introductory Course for Late-Arriving Cubans). One night—it was 3 A.M. already—Victor said to me, *"Yo ya no vengo más a este país. Tengo que saber a que vine. Tengo que hacer algo. Yo no vine a comer. No vine a traer una canastilla para nuestro niño. No quiero convertirme en una putica"* ("I'm not coming to this country anymore. I have to know why I came. I didn't come to eat. I didn't come to bring home things for the baby on the way. I don't want to become a little whore").

What crisis of conscience had I inspired by inviting Victor to the United States? I felt more than a little guilty that night. Victor and I, as a black man and a white woman, enact all the gender, race, and class distinctions that separate people in the two Cubas. Watching the *Bridges to Cuba* conference from his eyes, I noted his impatience with the heroic Cuban-American stories of return, of bravely flouting parental and exile community authority to go back to the island, of feeling linked to lost worlds, dreams, and affections. All the Cuban-Americans were dressed casually but well; lots of good wools, silks, and leather jackets. Victor had brought only the clothes on his back, a T-shirt and jeans. We spent the days after the conference going to thrift stores to buy clothes and shoes for him and his family. Every member of his extended family and many of his neighbors, he told me, expected a gift from him.

We spent a lot of time in bookstores, too. Victor impressed me with his vast knowledge of world literature, postmodern theory, and new trends in the study of gender and sexuality. It was clear to me he had put to good use the years he spent employed as a bibliographer in the National Library of Cuba. One day he saw a poster for a lecture on Isaac Bashevis Singer and suggested we attend. "You mean you've read Singer, too?" I asked, with too much surprise in my voice. "Of course I've read Singer," Victor retorted. "What, you think we haven't heard of Singer in Cuba?" When we arrived at the lecture hall, people shot questioning glances at this husky black man with shy eyes. Afterward, Victor was irritated: "Why was I the only black person there? Singer was a great writer." But, most of all, Victor knows poetry; and North American poetry, which he frequently translates into Spanish and can recite by heart, he knows best of all. Every poet, even the women I named, he'd read: Emily Dickinson, Elizabeth Bishop, Anne Sexton. Yes, yes, yes, he'd read them all.

Just before Victor left, he asked me to take him to a hardware store. On a Sunday afternoon I drove him to Ace Hardware, where he filled up his shopping cart with several kinds of glue—epoxy, adhesives, sticky substances that can bind the soles of shoes, seal leaking faucets, fix cracks. I said that it seemed as if he were trying to piece his life together. "Yes," he said, with a wry smile, "I've come unglued, *estoy despegado*."

Then I rushed Victor off to Borders Bookstore where Allen Ginsberg was signing copies of his poetry books. Going to see Ginsberg had also been Victor's idea. This time he was surprised when I admitted I'd never read anything by Ginsberg. "What, never read Ginsberg? He's my hero." We stood in a line that extended from one end of the travel section to the other. He didn't mind waiting, did he? I asked. Victor laughed and said it was a short line by Cuban standards. *Un pasatiempo dominical* (a Sunday recreation), he called it.

When our turn came, we each set our copies of *Howl* on the desk and watched as Ginsberg signed them. Ginsberg handed the books back to us and asked Victor where he was from. "Cuba," Victor said. "Did you know," replied Ginsberg, "that I was thrown out of Cuba when I went in 1965?" Victor told him that he knew, but assured him things were different now, assured him that he'd get a warm welcome from the poets of the younger generation. But what Victor, a Cuban poet of the African diaspora, most wanted to say to Ginsberg, a quintessential poet of the Jewish Diaspora, was that he's the poet he most admires, and that one day he's going to write a Cuban version of *Howl*, that will begin with the same lines, "I saw the best minds of my generation destroyed by madness, starving hysterical naked. . . ."

But there wasn't time for Victor to offer his tribute. Our moment with the great American rebel poet was over. Ginsberg, already forgetting us, was busy signing the next book.

CHAPTER 6

ANTHROPOLOGY THAT BREAKS YOUR HEART

*When I sit down to make my stories I know very well that
I want to take the reader by the throat, break her heart,
and heal it again. With that intention I cannot sort out
myself, say this part is for the theorist, this for the poet,
this for the editor, and this for the wayward ethnographer
who only wants to document my experience.*

—DOROTHY ALLISON, Skin: Talking
About Sex, Class, and Literature

But, you may say, if I don't want to be in Texas, why am
I here before a lectern in a hotel where the chandelier
dangles by a thread? I don't know if it's the immigrant in
me or the neurotic in me, but I am like that. Although I am
here, I imagine there is somewhere else I ought to be instead.
And so I don't stop tormenting myself: Is this where the voyage through the long tunnel leads? Is this why my parents
left Cuba?

I should try, as the Vietnamese Buddhist monk Thich
Nhat Hanh urges, to dwell in the present moment. As he
says, we ought not "to sacrifice the journey for the sake of the
arrival."[1] So I remind myself that I am here, at the meeting of
the American Ethnological Society, for a very good reason:
to defend the kind of anthropology that matters to me. It is
important to me that the meeting, this year, is organized by

a Chicano anthropologist, José Limón; that the incoming president of the American Ethnological Society, Renato Rosaldo, is also a Chicano anthropologist; that Latina/Latino anthropologists are (maybe for the first and last time) highly visible in the program; and that the theme of all our discussions is the border.

I am here because I am a woman of the border: between places, between identities, between languages, between cultures, between longings and illusions, one foot in the academy and one foot out. But I am also here because I have an intellectual debt to the Chicano critique of anthropology and the creative writing of Chicana authors. Beginning with Américo Paredes, it was Chicano and Chicana critics—not the Nuer—who turned around the anthropological mirror, questioning the way they had been represented by outsiders and offering their own, more complex and more lacerating representations, which made salient the question of who has the authority to speak for whom. It was the Chicano critique that wryly brought home the brutal role of subjectivity in cultural interpretation by pointing to the unreality and, even worse, the humorlessness of accounts written by Anglo anthropologists, who failed to understand when the natives were joking and when they were speaking seriously, and so produced parodies of the societies they intended to describe.[2] In turn, it was Chicana poets and writers who created new self-representations that not only included feminism but put the border on the map for all Latinas.[3]

I say I am here to "defend" the kind of anthropology that matters to me, which suggests that it is under attack. That may be too strong a way to put it, but lately there is tremendous anxiety that anthropology is becoming "activist art" overrun by "interpretive virtuosos."[4] And it is no exaggeration to say that anthropology is going through another terrible identity crisis.

There have been crises before, about anthropology's complicity with conquest, with colonialism, with functionalism, with realist forms of representation, with racism, with male domination. But the discipline has always managed to weather the storms and come out stronger, more inclusive, at once more vexed and more sure of itself.

This time, however, it may not recover so easily. There are serious problems. Many of them. For one thing, anthropology has lost exclusive rights over the culture concept, which was its birthright. The culture concept is now invoked not only across the disciplines, but far beyond the academy in an increasingly global society that is at pains to understand its various multiculturalisms.[5] Even anthropology's second-fiddle genre, the ethnography, has become the newly beloved form of a vast range of scholars, writers, artists, dancers, filmmakers, and talk show hosts. In our time, in this special period, this *periodo especial*, where bearing testimony and witnessing offer the only, and still slippery, hold on truth, every form of representation must pay homage to its roots in the ethnographic experience of talking, listening, transcribing, translating, and interpreting.

All this, you would think, should make anthropologists proud of themselves. How amazing—our vision of the world is actually *wanted* by the world. What incredible foresight we had, right? But the problem with such "appropriations" is that they threaten to leave anthropology without a place to hang its hat in the academy. The role that anthropology departments used to play as melting pots of vagabonds doing research in out-of-the-way places, where no one else wanted to go, is lately being filled by international institutes and area studies programs. And now that anthropologists have largely abandoned their old role as experts on the "origins" of our modern discontents, and too many of us are doing research at home, is there anything left that makes us unique? Has anthropology finally become dispensable?

The critics of the kind of anthropology that matters to me claim that the price anthropology must pay to survive into the next century is to become science, or risk becoming nothing. Anthropology has always stood uneasily on the border between the humanities and the sciences. But in recent years there are more anthropologists—and interested outsiders—who want to place the discipline squarely within the territory of science. It is not too late, they say. Anthropology can be "re-conquered" if its "grotesque tendencies"—postmodernist, feminist, relativist, multiculturalist—are reined in and anthropologists are enjoined "to abandon the pleasures of subjective narrativity for the fuddy-duddy rigors of empirical and statistical research."[6]

Clearly, there are important strategic reasons to induce anthropologists to re-fashion the discipline in ways that would allow it to pass better as science. Consider, as the 1994 Survey of Departments puts it, that "academic anthropology is a small discipline spread thinly across the land," with "only 16% of the nation's 2,157 colleges and universities presently offer[ing] an anthropology degree." Add to that the fact that, "in the academy, anthropology's size means that its programs are more vulnerable to changes than those of large disciplines, such as biology, psychology and history."[7]

Anthropology, what a vulnerable observer you are! You may well have to jump into the arms of the scientists if you are going to try to keep your grass hut in the academy.

B ut, you remind me, I am not in Texas to address anthropology's seduction by the scientists. No, I am here on a different mission—to defend the kind of anthropology that matters to me from the surprisingly ruthless criticism of the humanists.

The four panelists have spoken and now I must take the stage. I am to play the role of discussant. This means I must come up with something brilliant to say about some ordinary academic papers. Something dramatic. In only fifteen minutes. To help my cause, I have put on a red knit top, a long tight black skirt, and high-heeled sandals that tie at the ankles. I feel daring, ready for a bullfight, and just a little dizzy. I stayed up almost the entire night worrying and writing, rewriting and worrying, a woman in a hotel room in Texas, listening to the graceful waltz of my husband and son breathing in their sleep. I begin, in that academic voice I have learned to turn on and off, like a faucet:

"The essays you have heard today are grappling, in different ways, with the fundamental shift that has taken place in anthropology in the last decade—the shift toward viewing identification, rather than difference, as the key defining image of our theory and practice. Our classical dichotomies of Self and Other, Subject and Object, the West and the Rest have become hopelessly inadequate in the face of feminist and minority cultural critiques, the growing strength of various forms of 'native' anthropology, and the increasing borderization of our world. Yet the shift toward an intersubjective, Self-Self relation challenges the boundaries of anthropological discourse and raises some crucial questions: Is the turn toward identification going to lead us to ever more insular forms of anthropology? Even to anthropology's demise? On the other hand, on a less apocalyptic note, couldn't we say that the new focus on the possibilities and limits of identification is making anthropology finally and truly possible by leading us toward greater depth of understanding, greater depth of feeling about those whom we write about? Of course, 'feeling' is one of the subjects being contested in the presentations by literary critics Scott Michaelson and David Johnson, which urge us—not without feeling, I would add—to reconsider the role of the emotions not only in contemporary anthropology but in the academy and in cultural politics. This question of feeling, in turn, is related to the issues raised by the two anthropologists on the panel. To Jane Adams's question—to whom do we speak? And to Glen Perice's concern about the anxieties embedded in the relationships we form with our co-conspirators in the field. How might we speak so that we won't sell out to the dominant powers? Can we speak in a way that matters, in a way that will drive a wedge into the thick mud of business as usual?"

I look around the room. It is still quite early in the morning but there isn't a seat available. People are even standing in the back. The silence in the room is thick and heavy. Here and there, tucked among strangers, I see the familiar faces of colleagues, students, friends. I try to meet their gaze, to somehow show in a quick glance that I am grateful they have come, that I will do my best not to disappoint them. In those milliseconds when I am catching my breath, my eyes are scouring the entire room, trying to find him. The person I hope will hear these words. . . . No, he's not here. . . . It must be too painful. . . . But still I wish. . . . I turn to the far right corner and see José Limón, who looks more than a little apprehensive. But I look firmly in his direction and continue:

"When José Limón asked me to be the discussant for this panel, he warned me that the critique of Renato Rosaldo's work, from what he could gather of the abstracts, promised to be quite severe, even discomforting. Did I want to take it on? I didn't hesitate for a minute. If there was a strong challenge out there to Renato Rosaldo's work, and especially to his 'Grief and a Headhunter's Rage,' I needed to know about it. For me, 'Grief and a Headhunter's Rage' is a classical work of vulnerable writing carried out in the service of attaining the most profound ethnographic empathy possible. In that essay, Rosaldo asserts that he only came to fully understand the meaning of the rage in grief, which characterizes Ilongot headhunting in the Philippines, after the sudden tragic death of his wife, the anthropologist Michelle Zimbalist Rosaldo, while they were in the field. By courageously writing from his own grief, Renato Rosaldo returned to anthropology at a time when no return seemed possible."

I glance up and see Gabriel waving to me from the back of the room. What a wonderfully bright-eyed boy, a wonderfully long-legged boy. I wink at him and smile. He waves again, and as he leaves the room with David, I want to throw an invisible net around him, to protect him from all wounds, all hurts, all fears, all sadnesses. I think of Michelle Rosaldo, falling from the cliff to her death. Michelle was on her way to look over a new fieldwork site. She had good strong legs. She wasn't afraid. She expected to be back before nightfall. Renato had stayed in the old site with their two young sons. She told him to get the kids ready for bed. She'd be back to read them a story. But on the cliff, she lost her footing. And they came to tell Renato. And it was Renato who had to go find her at the bottom of the cliff. And yell at her for dying and not saying good-bye. And take her broken body to her Jewish grave in New York. And leave the Philippines. Leave and not return. And mourn. Mourn. By himself. For a long time. And then mourn with the Ilongots. In memory. With hindsight. And then mourn with other anthropologists, by writing an essay, unheard of until then in the history of anthropology, that is nothing less than an act of *shivah*—"to dwell with loss, to recover one's poverty, to be linked together in the presence of those absent and to give them . . . an everlasting name."[8]

"This is, obviously, a timely moment to discuss Renato Rosaldo's work in all its complexity and contradictions. As Renato now becomes president of the American Ethnological Society, his essay 'Grief and a Headhunter's Rage' marks its twelfth anniversary. Indeed, that essay was first delivered at a meeting of the American Ethnological Society. It is an essay that marked a turning point, not only for Rosaldo himself, but for anthropology, and certainly it deserves a most careful and engaged reading. I am grateful to Scott Michaelson and David Johnson for beginning that reading in their papers, and more generally for seeking to expand the boundaries of literary discourse by turning their analytical lens to an anthropological text. I welcome them to this meeting and hope their presence signals the beginning of more exchanges between anthropologists and literary critics."

I immediately feel foolish, like a hostess at the garden party of anthropology welcoming the foreign guests from the land of literary criticism and trying to put them at their ease. I try to smile in the direction of Michaelson and Johnson who glance back at me indifferently.

"Yet I disagree with many, indeed most, of the ways in which Michaelson and Johnson read Rosaldo's work. They accuse Rosaldo of ushering in a 'new sentimentalism' that is actually an old sentimentalism, says Michaelson, based in nineteenth-century Victorian women's culture, and anachronistic 'in the late twentieth century . . . after decades of Freudianisms, structuralisms, and post-structuralisms.' He feels—or rather thinks—that scholars in literature and anthropology are returning to questions that absorbed Nathaniel Hawthorne and Harriet Beecher Stowe, returning to universal humanist thinking. Johnson, in turn, finds suspect the recent turn toward viewing 'the former "objects" of ethnographical inquiry, cultural others, as being like us, subjects.' He feels—or rather thinks—that this trend toward doing away with the ideology of the transcendental observer is giving personal experience too much weight in ethnography. The difficulty is that personal experience, in his view, 'is what no one would be obliged to believe, to trust, perhaps not even to concede.'

"Although both Michaelson and Johnson read Rosaldo attentively, they have curiously chosen to disregard one of his central points—namely, the key role that the position of the observer plays in social analysis, including, I would think, literary analysis. Let me put it more colloquially: I want to know where Michaelson and Johnson are coming from. What is at stake for them in their critiques? I can only begin to guess at an answer to that question, since neither of them are reflexive about their own intellectual process and criticism. But reading them with feminist eyes, I am struck by the obvious—that here we have two men criticizing the work of another man who has made himself extremely vulnerable while refusing to make themselves vulnerable in how they read him. It is difficult not to invoke

Harold Bloom and the anxiety of influence. It is difficult not to see the Michaelson/Johnson critique in terms of the quintessential drama of the male writer's Oedipal slaying of powerful male literary precursors. It is difficult not to see in these critiques the desire of two young scholars to get 'a head' by decapitating a father—it would not, alas, be the first case of headhunting in the academy."

I know I'm being clever, even obnoxiously clever. Michaelson and Johnson look straight ahead, past me, past the audience.

"My interpretation is further complicated by the fact that Renato is a literary father who is self-consciously taking on feminist, even 'feminine' positions. He is cross-dressing as it were. In *Culture and Truth*, he is explicit in his critique of Max Weber's 'manly' ethic, which, as he puts it, 'underestimates the analytical possibilities of "womanly weaknesses" and "unmanly states,"' such as rage, feebleness, frustration, depression, embarrassment, and passion.'[9] Daring to speak of his sorrow, of his loss, his rage, daring, yes, to privilege sentiments, he dares to be 'feminine'—that is, feminine in the terms of our cultural logic and the way we ascribe genders to our writing. And immediately the sons come along to chastise him for not being *macho* enough."

Here I pause. I think I can drink something now, at this moment. But then I remember that I left my glass of ice water at the far end of the podium where I was sitting. I must keep going with a dry throat.

"The chastising is carried out in the name of Michelle Zimbalist Rosaldo. Michaelson writes that Renato views mourning as something that cannot be collapsed within ritual 'because emotions are primary, real, and fundamentally human.' Yet, with an almost wicked sense of righteousness, he points out that, in contrast, 'Michelle argues that emotions are produced in the first place through the mechanisms of routine and ritual.' He concludes, cruelly, I think, that Michelle's death 'finally permits' Renato 'to critique her.' And to wound just a little more, he adds that Michelle's death gives Renato a newfound sense of ethnographic authority, a sense that he is 'capable of feeling everything the Ilongot do. He recognizes their emotions, including their anger, within himself. . . . The experience of "rage" in grief is the same for both the Ilongot and Renato Rosaldo.' Johnson follows the same harsh path in his criticism. He insists that, regardless of the new turn toward subjectivity, 'anthropology needs an object' and that 'object' is Michelle Rosaldo's dead body. Her 'inert body guarantees the immediate repositioning of the subject, of the I of ethnography. . . . Over her dead body anthropology finds itself.' Listening to these crude words—especially for many here in the audience who knew Michelle Rosaldo—is terribly painful. One wants to mourn the use of such language, which resuscitates Michelle Rosaldo only to kill her for a second time. Yet both Michaelson and Johnson, I want to believe, have to believe, are trying desperately to imagine 'Grief and a Headhunter's Rage' from Michelle Rosaldo's perspective. I think they are sincere in feeling compelled to try to hear her voice, in defending the anthropology for which she stood, in seeking to keep the memory of her work alive."

My pulse is starting to race. I'm going to say what I've been holding back, what I think I've now earned the right to say after speaking intelligently and cleverly.

"Michelle Rosaldo's death had a huge impact on me. I was a graduate student, just back from a year of fieldwork in northern Spain, when news of her death reached us at Princeton. It terrified me. Gave me nightmares. I'd heard Michelle Rosaldo speak at Princeton just a year before—"

What I remember is this: she sat in the front of the long seminar table, patiently peeling an orange and eating it, segment by segment, as she spoke, and she caught my glance once and held it, hard, and I thought, she's not tender, she's of that generation of women that didn't get anything easy, and afterward I didn't try talking to her, I felt too weak, too uncertain about everything.

"And I thought—how could such a strong woman, such an important feminist anthropologist, die? And die like that, in the field, in that place charged with so much symbolism, that place where we, as women, become 'honorary males' and thus *macha* enough to gain acceptance into the anthropology club, which is so profoundly rooted in male quests and male musings about foreign lands?"

Yes, that was what had scared me most: that you could die doing fieldwork, that the danger of dying was real, because fieldwork is about nothing more primitive than confronting, with our contemporaries, our own mortality.

"We can only begin to imagine what direction feminist anthropology might have taken if Michelle Rosaldo were still alive today. And yet I don't think that Michaelson and Johnson do any service to Michelle Rosaldo in their efforts to resurrect her and pit her work on the emotions against the work of her grieving husband. The agency they grant her is patronizing, at best. And, at worst, Michaelson and Johnson are disrespectful and insensitive in the way they speak about her as merely a body. Renato, it seems to me, never, never does that—rather, in the process of mourning and healing he incorporates aspects of Michelle's life and work into his own life and work, including her feminism, her attention to the language of emotion, her concern to bridge the border between the private and the public. We must honor the dead, never walk on their tombs if we can help it."

Once, at Michigan, on my way to my office, on an especially gloomy day, I'd stopped and stared at the skulls in the paleoanthropology lab. Like a medieval ascetic, I brought my face close to a skull and pondered my own dissolution and thought of the legacy of the intellectual discipline to which I'd attached myself, this discipline which is so wrapped up with graves, with tombstones, with burial practices, with scraping away at layers upon layers of dead civilizations, with offerings left to those who are no longer with us, this discipline which, as Claude Lévi-Strauss put it in *Tristes Tropiques*, that most melancholy of ethnographies, is "so tormented by remorse."[10] Too often, when people find out I'm an anthropologist, they ask: "Have you dug up any interesting bones lately?"

"'Grief and a Headhunter's Rage' is itself a kind of tomb, a memorial to Michelle Zimbalist Rosaldo, and we must tread on it lightly. That essay, it seems to me, clearly marks the end of Rosaldo's sojourn as an anthropologist in the Philippines. Forced to part with Michelle, he also parts ways with the Ilongot, though he holds on to them both emotionally and intellectually. But that ending also marks a new beginning, a threshold for Renato, a return home. It is only after 'Grief and a Headhunter's Rage' that Renato comes out actively as a Chicano intellectual and develops his position as a theorist of the meaning of citizenship in the United States. He didn't do his research in the Philippines from a Chicano borderlands perspective, but rather from the perspective of a Harvard-trained anthropologist, very much influenced by a classical concept of culture which could only speak of natives in native lands, a concept of culture which was still inarticulate about borders. Anthropologists would only become articulate about borders thanks to the writing of Chicanas like Gloria Anzaldúa and Sandra Cisneros—who had to invent their own borderland anthropology in poetry, myths, and fictions because it didn't exist in the academy."

No, he hasn't come. . . . There's too much pain. I think I understand, but I don't. I still wish. . . . Later, they will tell me he sat in the lobby, alone, while I spoke.

"In my view, it isn't an accident that the effort to engage with the emotions in current anthropological and feminist writing follows upon Freudianisms, structuralisms, and poststructuralisms. I think what we are seeing are efforts to map an intermediate space we can't quite define yet, a borderland between passion and intellect, analysis and subjectivity, ethnography and autobiography, art and life. Consider, for example, the debate around Bill T. Jones's dance work 'Still/Here,' which was sparked by Arlene Croce's *New Yorker* essay where she announced she had refused to see the work on the grounds that his use of dancing inspired by the movements of HIV-positive dancers and video testimony by AIDS patients turned the art of dance into 'victim art,' a 'traveling medicine show.' As Homi Bhabha notes, what disturbs Croce about so-called 'Victim art' is that its effect is 'to solicit sympathy and collusion, rather than disinterested critical reading.'[11] The anxiety around such work is that it will prove to be beyond criticism, that it will be undiscussable. But the real problem is that we need other forms of criticism, which are rigorous yet not disinterested; forms of criticism which are not immune to catharsis; forms of criticism which can respond vulnerably, in ways we must begin to try to imagine."

On an airplane, a few months later—coming back from a conference in San Francisco about women's health, where I think I made myself extremely vulnerable by talking about my panic episode—I will sit next to a woman from Detroit whose mother was murdered. "Your mother murdered!" I will say, in a voice cracking with astonishment rather than with compassion. Yes, by the newspaper boy. Shot her. He was on drugs. I will look at the woman's face and ask: "But aren't you enraged? How do you live with the loss of your mother? How do you live with the fact that her murderer is still alive?" And she will say to me: "I belong to a group called Murder Victims Families for Reconciliation. I am against the death penalty. I have traveled up and down the California coast, talking to legislators, talking to victims, talking to teachers, teaching that you can't solve violence with more violence. You must forgive." This woman, I will think, is another angel in my path. Mourning, she reminds me, "is not replacing the dead but making a place for something else to be in relation to the past. . . . We bring the past to the present, we allow ourselves to experience what we have lost, and also what we are—that we are—despite this loss."[12] The

Ilongot, as I have learned from Renato Rosaldo, don't forgive. What they don't forgive is death. No, death cannot be forgiven. Can I be horribly honest? I am afraid. Too afraid to even imagine a headhunt.

"Michaelson asks: 'Of what value are sorrow and tears? How can one put them to use for purposes of a life politics?' Let me try to answer what is perhaps intended to be nothing more than a rhetorical question, a question for which no answer is really desired. I think of the film *Shoah*, which is a working through of sorrow, because all the tears have already been cried. Claude Lanzmann's aim is not to present gruesome images from the past, but to grapple with the impossibility of telling the story of the Holocaust. His effort is to 'screen loss.' He wants to make 'present in the film the absence of the dead.' Lanzmann returns with his camera to the prosaic sites where Jews passed from the normal world to the world of the camp. He goes back to the station building, the rails, the platforms, which are just as they were in 1942, not changed at all. 'I needed that,' Lanzmann says, 'a permanence of iron, of steel. I needed to attach myself to it.' He films survivors crossing the line between the world of the camp and the rest of the world. He films the distance, between present and past, the living and the dead. 'They can cross over, but neither they nor we are anywhere but in the present.'"[13]

No, we are nowhere but in the present. And I am here, in Texas, where I didn't think I wanted to be, but since I am here, I take a deep breath, and smile, and take joy that I am alive, and like a melodramatic soap opera star or maybe a country-western singer with a taut guitar, I look my audience in the eye and get ready to belt out those words I wrote very late at night when I was very tired and just wanted to get to sleep and forget everything. And I say:

"Call it sentimental, call it Victorian and nineteenth century, but I say that anthropology that doesn't break your heart just isn't worth doing anymore."

And I mean it. Really mean it. Because my heart is broken. Because the one person I wish had heard me sing this lament for him isn't here. Can't be here.

THE VULNERABLE OBSERVER

Anthropology That Breaks Your Heart

Create dangerously, for people who read dangerously. This is what I've always thought it meant to be a writer. Writing, knowing in part that no matter how trivial your words may seem, someday, somewhere, someone may risk his or her life to read them.

—EDWIDGE DANTICAT, Create Dangerously:
The Immigrant Artist at Work

So much has changed in anthropology in the last twenty-five years, since I was a young professor trying to find my voice in the academy. But my journey had begun long before then, as a graduate student. Anthropologists, I was taught, had to immerse themselves in the social worlds of other people while still maintaining distance and detachment. We were not to speak of ourselves or the things that made us unique observers, such as gender, race, class, nationality, and other markers of identity. And certainly we were not to be emotional in our writing.

I tried writing personally and poetically in my first anthropology graduate courses and kept getting Cs. A couple of professors expressed serious concern that I was "unteachable." I almost got thrown out of graduate school. But the thought of losing my scholarship was so frightening that I rushed to show them I was indeed very teachable. I forced myself to learn to conceal my presence in my writing and became adept at using academic language that would convey my supposed scientific objectivity. Immediately my grades improved. I was allowed to go on. Had I not altered my writing style, I'd never have become the anthropologist and professor I am today, nor would I have felt such an urgent need to write this book.

Nowadays most anthropologists, scholars, and writers are keenly aware of their self-positioning and speak openly of the emotional aspects of their work. Readers say this book played a key role in bringing about such a sea change. But in the 1990s, when I spoke of being vulnerable, colleagues would look at me funny, as if I'd let slip a profanity. Back in those days, the word "vulnerable" wasn't in wide circulation. Since the publication of this book in 1996, the usage of the word "vulnerable" has gone through a boom in the English language. We hear the word daily, referring to people, the environment, the planet. In anthropology alone, its usage has increased enormously. And an industry has emerged in "pop vulnerability" research, stressing the importance of feeling one's emotions fully. *The Vulnerable Observer* became part of the zeitgeist emerging at the end of the last century and helped to spur the word—and the concept of vulnerability—into our lexicon and our worldview today.

To my great gratitude, this book has found readers and been cited thousands of times. Scholars in anthropology and sociology draw from the book in qualitative research guides, handbooks, scholarly reflections, and ethnographies. *The Vulnerable Observer* is often mentioned as a pioneering model of the genre of "autoethnography," which surfaced in the 1970s and gained prominence in the 1990s and is now an accepted form of writing. I marvel at how the book has traveled across many disciplines, ranging from education studies to medicine, nursing, social work, and rhetoric; even in management studies it has found a wide readership.

Readers say the notion of "the vulnerable observer" put a label on something many anthropologists and other scholars had been grappling with: how to describe the practice of thinking through and laying bare one's subjectivity and personal connection to research. They point out that the book heightened the awareness of the emotional stakes of being an observer of any social world. Even readers less enamored of the approach described it as an appropriate way to do vulnerable work, incorporating only those personal disclosures that add to the ethnographic account and analysis, rather than distracting from it. I was fascinated to learn that many scholars borrow the book's title for their work, writing about "Trying to be a Vulnerable Observer" or "Reflections of a Vulnerable Observer" or "When Collecting Data Can Break Your Heart."

Beyond academic circles, the book has caught the attention of journalists, poets, writers, and casual readers. *The Vulnerable Observer* landed on a travel writer's list of "the best books that capture the complexities of writing about the real world." And the book has found its way onto more than a few syllabi. Something I never expected—students are asked to study it and write about it, and if that proves too burdensome, they can purchase a student essay about *The Vulnerable Observer* online. I was tempted to hunt for it myself, just out of curiosity, but thought it best not to in the end. Imagine if word got out that the author was buying a student essay about her own book!

Over the years, through letters, emails, and chance encounters, I've learned of students who've told me they decided to go into anthropology after reading this book. Though honored, I always feel a shiver. What if they regret it later? Should I tell them there are still plenty of scholars in academia who reject any kind of vulnerability? While the norms of academic writing have become more expansive and diverse, offering space for experimentation with form, I still encounter graduate students year after year in my seminar on ethnographic writing who feel stymied. They bemoan how they are being taught to maintain an impersonal approach in their writing that doesn't allow them to reflect on the way knowledge gets produced through a messy and often heart-wrenching entanglement with people whose lives you care about deeply.

I didn't seek to invent a new research method or transform the discipline of anthropology. I was attempting something more humble. In writing as I did, my simple wish was to find a way that I could exist in the academic world without destroying my spirit. Little did I know I wasn't the only one who felt this way. It turned out there were many of us who with much struggle and acute imposter syndrome had entered through the gates of the ivory tower only to discover we weren't willing to pay the price of belonging if it meant doing our research and writing in ways that deadened our souls.

Needing to convince myself that the spirit could be alive while doing rigorous intellectual work led me to produce a book with two impassioned titles. Truthfully, I couldn't decide which title to use: "The Vulnerable Observer" or "Anthropology That Breaks Your Heart." I'll never forget when Deb Chasman, then my editor at Beacon, said, "Why don't you use both titles?" I was glad to keep vulnerability *and* heartbreak. I felt we needed both in the academy. Trying to look at the world with distance and detachment had prevented too many of us from doing the work that really mattered.

B ecause I was born in Havana, the sea will always be my borderland. I find my way to the sea whenever I need inspira-
tion, though I find its infinite vastness terrifying. Years ago, there
were times when I was too afraid to go to the beach by myself. I
wrote several poems about those feelings in my bilingual book,
Everything I Kept/Todo lo que guardé, and in one of them, entitled
"Freedom," I wrote about a day when I finally went alone:

> *. . . I sat in the sand and opened my palms.*
> *I waited. I forgot I had been afraid. Soon I stopped waiting.*
>   *And felt freedom:*
> *Vast, huge, unknowable, ravishing.*
> *Divine.*

Looking back at these intense feelings, I am certain that being near the sea gave me the courage, and the freedom, to try
writing vulnerably, with an open heart, twenty-five years ago.

I was forty when I finished writing this book. In a rented
apartment gazing out at the sea on the southern tip of Miami
Beach, where I stayed with my husband, David, and my son,
Gabriel, who was then a boy, I made the final edits and revi-
sions. A photograph of me from that time makes me jealous of
my own lost youthfulness, how my neck was smooth, my arms
firm; I could wear a sleeveless dress without giving it a second
thought. Yet I felt old. I was afraid I hadn't accomplished any of
my dreams. I had wanted to be a writer but lost confidence in
my voice and had gone into anthropology instead.

I was drawn to anthropology's incessant journeys and vol-
untary periods of exile, its constant movement between places,
its desire to find magic and enchantment elsewhere, its wish to
champion and preserve endangered languages and cultures, its

commitment to supporting the struggles of those who suffer. To live between homes, between languages, between cosmologies, made sense to me. After all, I had been an immigrant child. That I could pursue this state of in-betweenness as a profession seemed incredible. The promise wasn't that you would find home. The promise was that you'd have unfettered consent to engage with the world in the manner that immigrants do—obsessively aware of impermanence, and grateful for moments of connection.

But that promise came with the expectation that you'd erase yourself and your feelings from your writing. It was an attitude that harkened back to the early days when anthropologists would have their appendix removed before going to do fieldwork in remote regions of the world. Such was their dedication, they were willing to dispose of an appendix to carry out fieldwork, not to mention enduring physical discomforts, illnesses like malaria, and other calamities. This heroic pride in possessing a hardy temperament made it taboo to want to be poetic and artistic. When famed anthropologist Ruth Benedict published her poems, she did so under a pseudonym.

That legacy was still going strong as this book took form. It left me wondering—Had I made a mistake in going into anthropology? Or could I be a writer and an anthropologist? I knew the essays in this book weren't the way I was supposed to write *as an anthropologist*. But I'd written in a voice that felt honest to me, a voice I didn't want to disguise under a pseudonym. Might I lose my job as a professor? And what would I do then? I had chosen to be part of the academic world, and it was in this world that I longed to create a space where I could be both an anthropologist and a writer.

I don't say this often, but I was also trying hard to be a philosopher. I'd been shunned by an undergraduate teacher, a philosophy professor I admired with devotion. It was after she declared I lacked the analytical mind to be a philosopher that I turned to anthropology. Better to pursue a career where I'd engage with real people in real places rather than with abstractions, I decided, but even after I'd chosen my path, I was haunted by the idea that I lacked some higher capacity of intelligence. Perhaps foolishly, I still wanted to believe my findings would address philosophical questions about the meaning of life.

The essays in this book reflected these conflicting desires. It wasn't quite anthropology. It wasn't quite creative writing. It wasn't quite philosophy. It was a book "too personal" to be anthropology, "too academic" to be creative writing, "not lofty enough" to be philosophy. It was a mix of all three, a mishmash, or to use the Cuban expression, *un arroz con mango*.

And my writing reflected all the entangled roles that made me the peculiarly vulnerable observer I was—an anthropologist and a scholar, and also a woman, wife, mother, daughter, granddaughter, niece, Jewish and Cuban, frequent traveler, bilingual speaker of Spanish and English. I was not going to leave out any part of myself. Yet only barely did I mention that I was married to a good man who did the laundry and didn't mind running errands and took our son to school each day and made dinner and washed dishes and left me free to read and write. His kindness was genuine, and I appreciated him, but sometimes, I knew, I didn't show it enough. There was guilt on his part too. I was the main breadwinner in our family. The weight on my shoulders was real. I absolutely could not lose my job. Plus, I was an immigrant with an existential dread of insecurity. Even so, rather than doing the traditional scholarly work expected of me, I was about to release a book about vulnerability and heartbreak, a book I feared anthropologists and academicians would dismiss as navel-gazing, the worst of condemnations.

I asked myself, *Was I going too far?*

Could I write about my grandfather's death in Miami Beach while writing about my research on death customs in Spain?

Could I write about the trauma suffered by Marta, a Mexican immigrant in Detroit, while writing about my frustration in botching the recording of my interview with her?

Could I write about the trauma I suffered when I was bedridden as an immigrant girl, a trauma that resurfaced in my adult life in the form of panic attacks and agoraphobia?

Could I write about the fraught nature of my relationship with Cuba, the island I've struggled so earnestly to reclaim?

Could I write about the wrenching experience of being on an academic panel where I defended Renato Rosaldo's telling of the untellable sorrow of losing his wife, Michelle Zimbalist Rosaldo, when they were doing fieldwork in the Philippines?

Could I write, in a phrase I nearly deleted, that anthropology that doesn't break your heart just isn't worth doing anymore?

I wanted someone to give me permission.

Then I realized I had to give myself permission.

Edwidge Danticat says we must create dangerously, imagining "someday, somewhere, someone may risk his or her life" to read the words we have set down on the page.

This was the writing that felt dangerous to me.

Holding my breath, I let the book go and hoped my words would find the readers who needed to read them as much as I needed to write them.

When we allow ourselves to be vulnerable, we open the door to creativity. Creativity isn't always valued in the academy, where scholasticism is too often preferred, but it is essential for discovering innovative ways of expressing ideas and sharing stories. I've come to realize that anthropology can be pursued in many voices, many genres, that we have limited ourselves to one form of prose writing when there are a wide range of possibilities for expressing the quest for meaning and human connection. I have told stories of my journeys as an anthropologist through poetry, memoir, fiction, photo-essay, and documentary film, restlessly seeking different ways of living and creating out of my vulnerability.

I think there are themes that haunt us throughout our lives and that we'll never let go of, themes we'll return to again and again, trying to gain clarity, another way of seeing and telling. The themes explored here—identity, cultural heritage, loss, memory, family, community, the search for home—reappear throughout my writing. I may think I am done with a story, but then I turn the kaleidoscope and peer inside and find a way to spin the tale anew.

This happened to me with the story of "the girl in the cast," which I told here from the perspective of the adult woman going through traumatic flashbacks and looking back on the experience of being bedridden as a child. Inexplicably, a few years ago, I felt the need to write it in the voice of Ruthie, the ten-year-old girl, letting the child tell her story. Because there was so much I wanted to imagine, rather than document, about that year of isolation and despair, I gave myself permission to tell the story as fiction. As I finished writing, I realized the novel I'd produced, *Lucky Broken Girl*, was young people's literature.

And so I've become an anthropologist who also writes for children. Two more works of fiction—a middle-grade novel, *Letters from Cuba*, and a picture book, *Tía Fortuna's New Home*—have followed. After having struggled to churn out academic prose, it gives me joy to write stories that can be enjoyed by children. But this writing isn't divorced from my years of research and travel. The anthropological gaze is present in stories that champion diversity, tolerance, heritage, and peaceful coexistence among people of all cultures and religions. While the turn to being a children's author happened through serendipity, it couldn't have come at a better time, as I have recently become a grandmother. I'm aware that I am writing for the next generation, for those like my granddaughter, who've come into the world during this moment of the pandemic, with all its anxiety and uncertainty, and one day will ask, Is there any life without vulnerability?

Despite all the ways I've interrogated anthropology, despite not always feeling proud of being an anthropologist, despite having called ethnographic writing "a second-fiddle genre," despite having gone on to write poetry, memoir, and fiction, I am an anthropologist at heart. An anthropologist not in the credentialed or academic sense but in the sense that I have cared, and will always care, about vulnerability as a shared experience and the way profound and unfathomable encounters can take place between strangers that will change our lives forever.

One such experience happened a few years ago, in 2019, when I was last in Spain. The village of Santa María, because it was the place of my first fieldwork, lives very vividly in my imagination, and I've returned many times over the years. I won't ever forget alighting there as a naïve anthropologist at the age of twenty-one, only knowing I had come to witness the lives of people who had the power to wrest food from the land and still felt ashamed for not having left for the city. Forty-one years after my first visit, I sought out the villagers I'd known in my youth, the few still alive. I teared up at the sight of them, and they at the sight of me. *Cómo pasa el tiempo*, how the years pass, we agreed.

Then David and I went to the city of León for tapas and drinks with Fran Llamazares, a self-made local historian who has created a website to honor the village. A young man came in while we were at the bar. Fran introduced Tonio as being from Santa María, a grandson of Amparo, who I knew from the village. But I didn't know Tonio. He'd grown up in Madrid, taken there by his parents who were part of the rural exodus to the cities, and had married, had a child, and become a chef. He wanted a change and had returned to live in León with his family. He planned to renovate his grandmother Amparo's house, forgotten for years, and move to the village.

I was intrigued by this idea of reverse migration, and we dove into a lively conversation. After a while, I asked Fran and Tonio if I could photograph them. It was only then that I took a close look at Tonio's tattoos. On his right arm, he'd tattooed "the Chef," but on his left arm I saw an image that looked familiar. It was Amparo in her black widow's dress, which was her permanent attire, sifting kernels of wheat with one of the hand-made wooden sieves that were still used back in those days and later found their way into the ethnographic museum. As Tonio held up his left arm and showed me on his cell phone the image that the tattoo had been modeled on, I realized why it was familiar. I had taken the photograph!

The photograph was from 1984, when I took pictures with a square format Rollei. I loved that camera. It allowed me to look down into the viewfinder and then look up and gaze into the eyes of the person I was photographing. I always enlarged the pictures and gave them to the people I photographed. I never imagined that one of these photographs would end up etched into the flesh of a grandson who'd grown up in the city, far from the rural life of a grandmother I came to know through my fieldwork. Tonio was searching for home, just as I was through my anthropology. I had not expected my work to serve as a map back to an abandoned ancestral home that had acquired new meaning for a new generation. Here it was, the sense of possibility, the confluence of past, present, and future, the interconnectedness that anthropology had promised me. I was far from the ocean, in the emptied region of Spain, where village after village awaits its lost grandchildren, far from my borderland, but Tonio's journeys and mine had flowed into each other and landed on the same shore.

When I think back to the many strangers who trusted me with their stories, opened their homes to me, told me their dreams, I feel grateful for how they gave me a lighthouse within myself, so I would always remember, in dark moments, that I am not alone in the world. Even without a map, I was not to be afraid, I would not be lost, I would find my way. I know I didn't offer anything quite as spectacular in return. There was sorrow in their lives I couldn't heal or mend, but I could listen, I could be alive with them. Life, life. *Vida, vida.*

As I finish my epilogue, a new year has begun, and most of all I wish for this book to embolden you, reader, to think and write in a way you didn't imagine was possible. Perhaps this small effort to create dangerously can speak to the inchoateness of what we're experiencing in these times and inspire you to see beyond what we can see with our eyes.

I could never have imagined how intensely relevant vulnerability would become in our era, how heartbreak would be an all-too-familiar condition. There is no better moment to be a vulnerable observer than now and to embark on an anthropology—or any close-up study of people—that unlocks hidden truths about our shared humanity, our shared mortality. More than ever, I believe writing with a broken heart is the path towards understanding what we cannot yet name, what the sea has not yet swept away.

—Ann Arbor, Michigan,
February 2022

ACKNOWLEDGMENTS

The essays in this book were written between 1987 and 1996. During these years my spirit and my writing have been nurtured by friends and colleagues in many fields. I am especially grateful for the faith given me by Ester Shapiro Rok, who encouraged me to believe that these essays might be creative writing and inspired me with her own thinking and writing about grief. María de los Angeles Torres always keeps me honest about Cuba, gently debriefing me on so many occasions. To Deborah Gordon I owe some of the most profound insights I have about myself as an anthropologist. Alan West has taught me to be a better poet. My essay on "The Girl in the Cast" would not have seen the light of day without the support and knowledge of Gelya Frank, Marianne Gullestad, Sandra Cisneros, Joanne Leonard, Susan Gelman, and Bruce Mannheim. I have been fortunate over the years to have James Fernandez, José Limón, Renato Rosaldo, and Victor Perera as caring mentors. Teofilo Ruiz and Scarlett Freund gave me absolutely essential comments, as only old friends can give, just before I let this book go. To all my deepest thanks.

My debt to those who allowed me to enter into their lives, knowing I would write about them, will never be fully repaid. I cannot, ever, make myself vulnerable enough.

I have been blessed with generous fellowship support from the MacArthur Foundation, the Harry Frank Guggenheim Foundation, the Lucius Littauer Foundation, the Council for International Exchange of Scholars, and most recently from the John Simon Guggenheim Foundation. At the University of Michigan I received grants from the International Institute, the Office of the Vice President for Research, and the Rackham School of Graduate Studies. This book was completed during a joyful period as a Rockefeller Residence Fellow at the Cuban Research Institute of Florida International University.

To my husband, David Frye, and my dear son, Gabriel, my thanks for their love and patience and for sleeping soundly while I wrote late into the night. And a special thank-you to Gabriel, who is teaching me so much with his own great big heart.

Deb Chasman, my editor at Beacon Press, had an inspired vision of how this book would tell its story. To *la editora suprema*, I dedicate this book, *con el corazón en la mano*.

—Miami Beach
April 1996

2022 Acknowledgments: With warmest thanks to Sandra Cisneros, Marjorie Agosín, and Lucía Suarez for offering wise comments on the new epilogue; to Miranda Garcia for her research on the book's reception; and to Helene Atwan and the team at Beacon Press for giving this book a chance at rebirth.

NOTES

1. The Vulnerable Observer

1. Isabel Allende, *Paula* (New York: HarperCollins Publishers, 1995), 238, 310. Also see my review, "In the House of Spirits," in *Women's Review of Books* 13, 2 (November 1995): 8. Allende's story "Of Clay We Are Created" appears in *The Stories of Eva Luna* (New York: Macmillan, 1991).

2. Clifford Geertz, *After the Fact: Two Countries, Four Decades, One Anthropologist* (Cambridge, Mass.: Harvard University Press, 1995).

3. George Devereux, *From Anxiety to Method in the Behavioral Sciences* (The Hague: Mouton, 1967), 6, 84.

4. Clifford Geertz, *Works and Lives: The Anthropologist as Author* (Stanford, Calif.: Stanford University Press, 1989), 5–6.

5. Geertz, *After the Fact*, 44.

6. Kay Redfield Jamison, *An Unquiet Mind* (New York: Alfred A. Knopf, 1995), 7.

7. Jamison, *An Unquiet Mind*, 188–189, 203.

8. Jamison, *An Unquiet Mind*, 212–213.

9. Alice Kaplan, *French Lessons: A Memoir* (Chicago: University of Chicago Press, 1994); Carolyn Kay Steedman, *Landscape for a Good Woman: A Story of Two Lives* (New Brunswick, N.J.: Rutgers University Press, 1987); José E. Limón, *Dancing with the Devil: Society and Cultural Poetics in Mexican-American South Texas* (Madison: University of Wisconsin Press, 1994).

10. Patricia J. Williams, *The Alchemy of Race and Rights* (Cambridge, Mass.: Harvard University Press, 1991).

11. Daphne Patai, "Sick and Tired of Nouveau Solipsism," Point of View essay in *The Chronicle of Higher Education* (February 23, 1994).

12. Ruth Behar, *Translated Woman: Crossing the Border with Esperanza's Story* (Boston: Beacon Press, 1993).

13. See Gelya Frank, "Ruth Behar's Biography in the Shadow: A Review of Reviews," *American Anthropologist* 97, 2 (1995): 357–359, for an account of the controversy surrounding this chapter.

14. See the discussion of this point in Kamala Visweswaran, *Fictions of Feminist Ethnography* (Minneapolis: University of Minnesota Press, 1994), 8.

15. See the lucid discussion of representation in Michael S. Roth, *The Ironist's Cage: Memory, Trauma, and the Construction of History* (New York: Columbia University Press, 1995), 224.

16. The quotation, from Graham Good, is cited in Ruth-Ellen Boetcher Joeres and Elizabeth Mittman, eds., *The Politics of the Essay: Feminist Perspectives* (Bloomington: Indiana University Press, 1993), 20. This collection offers an excellent discussion of the essay as a feminist genre. In anthropology, the essay has been innovatively used by Clifford Geertz, *The Interpretation of Cultures* (New York: Basic Books, 1973); James Clifford, *The Predicament of Culture: Twentieth-Century Ethnography, Literature, and Art* (Cambridge, Mass.: Harvard University Press, 1988); and Renato Rosaldo, *Culture and Truth: The Remaking of Social Analysis* (Boston: Beacon Press, 1989). It has been championed as an ideal form for the new experimental ethnography by George E. Marcus, "Contemporary Problems of Ethnography in the Modern Worlds System," in James Clifford and George E. Marcus, eds., *Writing Culture: The Poetics and Politics of Ethnography* (Berkeley and Los Angeles: University of California Press, 1986), 191. In turn, in *Fictions of Feminist Ethnography*, pp. 11–12, Kamala Visweswaran makes the argument that the essay is a crucial medium for feminist ethnography.

17. On Malinowski and fiction, see Clifford, *The Predicament of Culture*, 92–113, and Visweswaran, *Fictions of Feminist Ethnography*, 4–5.

18. Later, I went on to write about Spain in relation to other losses and absences. The silencing of my Sephardic identity is the subject of my essay "The Story of Ruth, the Anthropologist," in Jeffrey Rubin-Dorksy and Shelley Fisher Fishkin, eds., *The People of the Book* (Madison: University of Wisconsin Press, 1996).

19. Gloria Anzaldúa, *Borderlands / La Frontera: The New Mestiza* (San Francisco: Aunt Lute Books, 1987), 3.

20. Earlier, I'd written about my daughter's guilt about my mother's hysterectomy. See "The Body in the Woman, the Story in the Woman," in Laurence A. Goldstein, ed., *The Female Body: Figures, Styles, Speculations* (Ann Arbor: University of Michigan Press, 1991).

21. Bill T. Jones, with Peggy Gillespie, *Last Night on Earth* (New York: Pantheon Books, 1995), 246.

22. Barbara Browning, *Samba: Resistance in Motion* (Bloomington and Indianapolis: Indiana University Press, 1995): x.

23. See H. David Brumble III, *American Indian Autobiography* (Berkeley and Los Angeles: University of California Press, 1988), and Arnold Krupat, *For Those Who Come After: A Study of Native American Autobiography* (Berkeley and Los Angeles: University of California Press, 1985). For more general discussion, see Judith Okely and Helen Callaway, eds., *Anthropology and Autobiography* (New York: Routledge, 1992).

24. Elisabeth Burgos-Debray, *I, Rigoberta Menchú: An Indian Woman in Guatemala* (New York: Schocken Books, 1984).

25. Cherríe Moraga and Gloria Anzaldúa, eds., *This Bridge Called My Back: Writings by Radical Women of Color* (New York: Kitchen Table, Women of Color Press, 1981); Henry Louis Gates, Jr., ed., *Bearing Witness: Selections from African-American Autobiography in the Twentieth Century* (New York: Pantheon Books, 1991).

26. On changing ideas of the "native" in anthropology, see the essays in Ruth Behar and Deborah A. Gordon, eds., *Women Writing Culture* (Berkeley and Los Angeles: University of California Press, 1995). The quotation from Geertz is in his *Interpretation of Cultures*, p. 452.

27. Among key works, see Susan N. G. Geiger, "Women's Life Histories: Method and Content," *Signs* 11 (1986): 334–351; Bella Brodzki and Celeste Schenck, eds., *Life/Lines: Theorizing Women's Autobiography* (Ithaca, N.Y.: Cornell University Press, 1988); Personal Narratives Group, eds., *Interpreting Women's Lives: Feminist Theory and Personal Narratives* (Bloomington: Indiana University Press, 1989); Joanne M. Braxton, *Black Women Writing Autobiography: A Tradition Within a Tradition* (Philadelphia: Temple University Press, 1989); Nancy K. Miller, *Getting Personal: Feminist Occasions and Other Autobiographical Acts* (New York: Routledge, 1991).

28. Sandra Harding, *Feminism and Methodology* (Bloomington: Indiana University Press, 1987).

29. Donna J. Haraway, "Situated Knowledges: The Science Question in Feminism and the Privilege of Partial Perspective," in her *Simians, Cyborgs, and Women: The Reinvention of Nature* (New York: Routledge, 1991), 196.

30. Jane Tompkins, "Me and My Shadow," in Diane P. Freedman and Olivia Frey, eds., *The Intimate Critique: Autobiographical Literary Criticism* (Durham, N.C.: Duke University Press, 1993).

31. Susan Rubin Suleiman, *Risking Who One Is: Encounters with Contemporary Art and Literature* (Cambridge, Mass.: Harvard University Press, 1994).

32. Toril Moi, *Simone de Beauvoir: The Making of an Intellectual Woman* (Cambridge, Mass.: Blackwell Publishers, 1994), 218.

33. Moi, *Simone de Beauvoir*, 225.

34. Moi, *Simone de Beauvoir*, 250–252.

35. Margaret Randall, "Who Lies Here?" (manuscript, 1996).

2. Death and Memory

This essay was awarded Honorable Mention by the Stirling Committee for contributions in psychological anthropology at the American Anthropological Association annual meeting in 1989.

1. Fifty years ago nearly half the population was employed in farmwork. At present, only about 15 percent still works on the land, 12 percent being small peasant farmers like those of Santa María, who are rapidly aging and approaching death. José Felix Tezanos, "Transformaciones en la estructura social española," in Francesc Hernández and Francesc Mercadé, eds., *Estructuras sociales y cuestión nacional en España* (Barcelona: Ariel, 1986), 52–53.

2. Cited in Luis Carlos Sen Rodríguez, "¿Hacia un nuevo compartamiento social?," in *Diario de León*, series on "La guerra civil española en León," Part II, fascículo 12 (1987): 349.

3. Raymond Williams, *The Country and the City* (London: Chatto and Windus, 1973), 297.

4. See Raymond Carr and Juan Pablo Fusi Aizpurua, *Spain: Dictatorship to Democracy* (London: George Allen & Unwin, 1979).

5. Victor Pérez Díaz, *El retorno de la sociedad civil* (Madrid: Instituto de Estudios Económicos, 1987), 404, 442.

6. Miguel Delibes, *Vivir al día* (Barcelona: Ediciones Destino, 1968), 115; also see Carr and Fusi Aizpurua, *Spain*, 68.

7. Luis Buñuel, *Mi último suspiro* (Barcelona: Plaza y Janés, 1982), 14.

8. Barbara Myerhoff, *Number Our Days* (New York: Simon and Schuster, 1978), 74–75.

9. The image of the dying village, common to much of Southern Europe, should not be exaggerated. The initial, and seemingly final, desertion of the villages was followed, in the late 1970s and 1980s, by a nostalgic return to the countryside, with emigrants spending their hard-earned urban cash to renovate old farmhouses to use as weekend and summer homes. In many places, old traditions and fiestas were revitalized, as folklore or as rituals of reversion. See James Fernandez,

"The Call to the Commons" (paper presented at the Oxford Conference on Forms of Reciprocity and Cooperation in Rural Europe, St. Anthony's College, September 8–11, 1981), on the former; Rayna Rapp, "Ritual of Reversion: On Fieldwork and Festivity in Haute Provence," *Critique of Anthropology* 6 (1986): 35–48, on the latter. And, in Santa María as elsewhere, a handful of younger families who stayed in the village began to work the land on a larger scale, with machinery. Even the emigrants always returned to lend a hand in the old family economy, whether in the harvest of wheat and rye preceding the village fiesta, which was its celebration, or the slaughter of the family pig on Saint Martin's Day. But none of those who returned, then or now, expected to return to agriculture or to village life on a permanent basis. For the emigrants, who were in the majority, the village became a temporary oasis, where one could get a respite from crowded apartments and cities, and where the grandchildren, blissfully ignorant of how to plow a field or milk a cow, could spend their days cruising the streets on their bicycles.

10. Walter Benjamin, *Illuminations*, 2nd edition (New York: Schocken Books, 1978), 255.

11. Pierre Nora, "Between Memory and History: Les Lieux de Mémoire," *Representations*, special issue on "Memory and Counter-Memory," 26 (spring 1989): 7.

12. Nora, "Between Memory and History," 13–14.

13. Nora, "Between Memory and History," 16.

14. Philippe Ariès, *The Hour of Our Death* (New York: Alfred A. Knopf, 1981), 569.

15. Ariès, *The Hour of Our Death*, 28.

16. Ariès, *The Hour of Our Death*, 16; Richard Huntington and Peter Metcalf, *Celebrations of Death: The Anthropology of Mortuary Ritual* (Cambridge: Cambridge University Press, 1979), 204.

17. Ruth Behar, "The Struggle for the Church: Popular Anticlericalism and Religiosity in Post-Franco Spain," in Ellen Badone, ed., *Religious Orthodoxy and Popular Faith in European Society* (Princeton, N.J.: Princeton University Press, 1990).

18. Ariès, *The Hour of Our Death*, 563.

19. In the Alto Minho of Portugal, where a cross is also marked on the bread as it rises, Pina-Cabral notes that "bread is used as a symbol of community created through the unity of commensality: a form of commensality which sustains life, both physically and spiritually." See Joao de Pina Cabral, *Sons of Adam, Daughters of Eve: The Peasant Worldview of the Alto Minho* (Oxford: Clarendon Press, 1986), 42.

Thus, in rural Portugal as in rural Spain, people say that "bread is sacred," a notion that is probably widespread in Southern Europe where bread has long been the staple of the rural diet. In Sardinia, for example, there is a proverb, "One who has bread never dies." See Carole M. Counihan, "Bread as World: Food Habits and Social Relations in Modernizing Sardinia," *Anthropological Quarterly* 57, 2 (1984): 50.

20. The link between bread and wine, community and Christ that was established at death was carried over into other rituals. One such ritual known as "making the offering" involved the female kin of the deceased who, during the offertory at mass every Sunday, would kneel at the foot of the altar, receiving the "Our Father" that the priest said in memory of the deceased and lighting a candle in the dead person's memory. This offering was made during an entire year, in Sunday mass after Sunday mass, with the village community bearing witness to the remembrance of the departed; for this offering, the priest was "given" one or two bushels of wheat by the family of the deceased. Similarly, on All Saints' Day, women brought to mass offerings of wheat, in baskets surrounded by lit candles, so that the priest might convert the staff of life into masses for the dead.

21. Maurice Bloch and Jonathan Parry, eds., *Death and the Regeneration of Life* (Cambridge: Cambridge University Press, 1982), 3–5.

22. Sandra Ott, *The Circle of Mountains: A Basque Shepherding Community* (Oxford: Clarendon Press, 1981).

23. Behar, "The Struggle for the Church."

24. Jacques le Goff, *The Birth of Purgatory* (Chicago: University of Chicago Press, 1984).

25. See Natalie Zemon Davis, "Ghosts, Kin, and Progeny: Some Features of Family Life in Early Modern France," *Daedalus* 102, 2 (1977): 87–114, for an interesting discussion of "the Catholic mutual economy of salvation." With its strong links to corporate institutions, Catholic mortuary customs, in sixteenth- and seventeenth-century France, were in tension with the deritualized Protestant approach to death that did away with the dead as an "age group," focusing instead on "the family arrow moving ahead in the world." This shift seems similar to that which has taken place in rural Spain more recently. However, as the rest of the text indicates, the idea of "the family arrow" is being challenged by younger Catholics who are redefining the domain of the corporate.

26. See Ruth Behar, *The Presence of the Past in a Spanish Village: Santa María del Monte* (Princeton, N. J.: Princeton University Press, 1986; revised edition, 1991).

27. I realize that in other Spanish settings, like rural Galicia, which has traditionally had niche-like burial chapels, niches may have nothing to do with a symbolic recognition of the end of farm life. Among early Christians the dead were often buried in caves, and certainly it has been common for centuries to bury the dead in the walls of churches or, in the case of the Spanish kings, in the walls of the Escorial. But I would argue that for this region of Spain, where such niches are a new phenomenon, they represent a radical departure from previous styles of burial, and therefore call for interpretation in light of recent historical and cultural transformations.

28. For historical background, see Judith Laikin Elkin, *Jews of the Latin American Republics* (Chapel Hill: University of North Carolina Press, 1988), and Robert M. Levine, *Tropical Diaspora: The Jewish Experience in Cuba* (Gainesville: University Press of Florida, 1993).

29. This sitting "to the earth," that is, closer to the ground than usual, serves as "a physical adjustment to one's emotional state, a lowering of the body to the level of one's feelings, a symbolic enactment of remorse and desolation." See Maurice Lamm, *The Jewish Way in Death and Mourning* (New York: Jonathan David Publishers, 1969), 112.

30. It was with shock that I learned, on July 14, 1988, of being named a MacArthur fellow: a year after my grandfather died, and on the very day he died. I want to dedicate this fellowship to his name and use it to explore the strange paths of death, history, and memory.

31. Robert N. Bellah, Richard Madsen, William M. Sullivan, Ann Swidler, and Steven M. Tipton, *Habits of the Heart: Individualism and Commitment in American Life* (Berkeley and Los Angeles: University of California Press, 1985), 153.

32. James Clifford has written of the pervasiveness of "the theme of the vanishing primitive" in ethnographic writing. Ways of life do disappear, populations are displaced and sometimes destroyed, and traditions can be lost, as Clifford points out; yet, he questions what he calls "the allegory of salvage." This is a persistent form of narrative structure by which the anthropologist captures and codifies, authorizes and redeems the disappearing past in the text that inscribes that disappearance. See James Clifford, "On Ethnographic Allegory," in James Clifford and George E. Marcus, eds., *Writing Culture: The Poetics and Politics of Ethnography* (Berkeley and Los Angeles: University of California Press, 1986), 112–113. Similarly, Renato Rosaldo has called our attention to the "imperialist nostalgia" that grips agents of

colonialism (including, in subtle ways, anthropologists), who "mourn the passing of what they themselves have transformed"; see Renato I. Rosaldo, "Imperialist Nostalgia," in his *Culture and Truth: The Remaking of Social Analysis* (Boston: Beacon Press, 1989), 69.

33. Nora, "Between Memory and History," 12.

34. Michel de Certeau, *The Practice of Everyday Life* (Berkeley and Los Angeles: University of California Press, 1984), 86–87.

35. I owe this insight to Loring Danforth, whose encouragement was crucial during the writing of this essay. In addition to being dedicated to my two grandfathers, this essay is also dedicated to Justa Llamazares, who died during the summer of 1989. Justa was one of the people I most loved in Santa María. She was soft-spoken, good to the core, and a sharp social analyst. She was, also, a religious virtuosa. In the pro-Catholic climate of the early Franco years, when, ironically, passing families of gypsies were no longer allowed to take refuge in the portal of the village church, it was Justa who opened the doors of her house to the family of a gypsy woman who had just given birth and was hemorrhaging. She was one of the people whose doors were always open to the errant anthropologist, and I will miss her.

36. Johannes Fabian, "How Others Die—Reflections on the Anthropology of Death," in Arien Mack, ed., *Death in American Experience* (New York: Schocken Books, 1973), 198.

37. See Renato I. Rosaldo, "Grief and a Headhunter's Rage: On the Cultural Force of Emotions," in his *Culture and Truth*; Renato I. Rosaldo, "Death in the Ethnographic Present," in Paul Hernadi, ed., *The Rhetoric of Interpretation and the Interpretation of Rhetoric* (Durham, N.C.: Duke University Press, 1989); Loring M. Danforth, *The Death Rituals of Rural Greece* (Princeton, N.J.: Princeton University Press, 1982).

38. Alvin H. Rosenfeld, *Double Dying: Reflections on Holocaust Literature* (Bloomington: Indiana University Press, 1980), 14.

39. Judith Laiken Elkin, "Recoleta: Civilization and Barbarism in Argentina," *Michigan Quarterly Review* 27, 2 (1988): 237.

40. Michael Taussig, *Shamanism, Colonialism, and the Wild Man: A Study in Terror and Healing* (Chicago: University of Chicago Press, 1987). My thanks to Renato Rosaldo for suggesting the contrast between the rhetorical strategies of Elkin and Taussig.

41. de Certeau, *The Practice of Everyday Life*, 191.

42. de Certeau, *The Practice of Everyday Life*, 195.

43. Cited in Rosenfeld, *Double Dying*, 18–19.

4. The Girl in the Cast

1. Carol Becker, *The Invisible Drama: Women and the Anxiety of Change* (New York: Macmillan, 1982), 14–17. My warm thanks to Nereida Garcia-Ferraz for sharing this important book with me.

2. Alice Miller, *The Drama of the Gifted Child* (New York: Basic Books, 1990).

3. Marjorie Leonard, "Fear of Walking in a Two-and-a-Half-Year-Old Girl," *Psychoanalytic Quarterly* 28 (1959): 29–39.

4. Henry Louis Gates, Jr., "A Giant Step," *New York Times Magazine*, December 9, 1990, 34–35.

5. Oliver Sacks, *A Leg to Stand On* (New York: Harper and Row, 1984), 134–135, 156–157, 161–162.

6. There is more than a little of masculine heroics in Oliver Sacks's story. The women in his story are primarily nurses and assistants.

7. Carol Gilligan, "Joining the Resistance: Psychology, Politics, Girls and Women," *Michigan Quarterly Review*, special issue on "The Female Body," 29, 4 (1990): 512. Reprinted in Laurence A. Goldstein, ed., *The Female Body: Figures, Styles, Speculations* (Ann Arbor: University of Michigan Press, 1991).

8. Dana Crowley Jack, *Silencing the Self: Women and Depression* (Cambridge, Mass.: Harvard University Press, 1991).

9. Gilligan, "Joining the Resistance," 531.

10. Judith Stacey, "On Resistance, Ambivalence and Feminist Theory: A Response to Carol Gilligan," *Michigan Quarterly Review* 29, 4 (1990): 537–546. Reprinted in Goldstein, *The Female Body*.

11. Richard N. Coe, *When the Grass Was Taller: Autobiography and the Experience of Childhood* (New Haven, Conn.: Yale University Press, 1984), 9.

12. Sandra Cisneros, *The House on Mango Street* (New York: Random House, 1991, orig. 1989), 80, 88–89, 108.

13. Phone conversation with Sandra Cisneros, March 3, 1992. In addition to talking at length with me about her work, Sandra Cisneros kindly gave me permission to read the diaries she kept from the age of thirteen to age fifteen, which I hope to write about in more detail on another occasion.

14. Salman Rushdie, "Imaginary Homelands," in his *Imaginary Homelands: Essays and Criticism 1981–1991* (New York: Viking Penguin, 1992), 9–10.

15. James Olney, remarks at a workshop on "The Construction of Childhood," held in Trondheim, Norway, 1992. See the proceedings

of the workshop in Marianne Gullestad, ed., *Imagined Childhoods* (Oslo: Scandinavian University Press, 1996).

16. Recently, there have been pleas for a more autobiographical anthropology, rooted in embodied knowledge, in which the distinction between self and other becomes blurred. See Judith Okely and Helen Callaway, eds., *Anthropology and Autobiography*.

5. *Going to Cuba*

1. Carmelita Tropicana, "Milk of Amnesia / Leche de Amnesia," *TDR: The Journal of Performance Studies* 39, 3 (fall 1995): 105.

2. David Rieff, *The Exile: Cuba in the Heart of Miami* (New York: Simon and Schuster, 1993).

3. Here one could cite a vast literature, but see especially Linda Basch, Nina Glick Schiller, and Cristina Szantaon Blanc, *Nations Unbound: Transnational Projects, Postcolonial Predicaments, and Deterritorialized Nation-States* (Basel, Switzerland: Gordon and Breach Publishers, 1994). Of special interest is the preface by Khachig Tololyan, "The Nation-State and Its Others: In Lieu of a Preface," to the first issue of the journal *Diaspora* (*Diaspora* 1, 1[1991]: 3–7). An excellent, recent discussion of the idea of diaspora in the Cuban context can be found in Maria de los Angeles Torres, "Encuentros y Encontronazos: Homeland in the Politics and Identity of the Cuban Diaspora," *Diaspora* 4, 2 (fall 1995): 211–238.

4. Rieff, *The Exile*, 33, 50–51, 100.

5. Daniel Boyarin and Jonathan Boyarin, "Diaspora: Generation and the Ground of Jewish Identity," *Critical Inquiry* 19 (summer 1993): 716, 718, 723.

6. Philip Roth, *Operation Shylock: A Confession* (New York: Simon and Schuster, 1993).

7. Sidra DeKoven Ezrahi, "'Diasporism': Philip Roth from 'Portnoy' to 'Shylock'" (manuscript, 1994).

8. Paul Gilroy, *The Black Atlantic: Modernity and Double-Consciousness* (Cambridge, Mass.: Harvard University Press, 1993).

9. Stuart Hall, "Cultural Identity and Cinematic Representation," *Framework* (University of Warwick Arts Federation) 36 (1989): 74–76.

10. Ruth Behar, ed., *Bridges to Cuba / Puentes a Cuba* (Ann Arbor: University of Michigan Press, 1995).

11. Rudolfo A. Anaya and Francisco Lomeli, eds., *Aztlán: Essays on the Chicano Homeland* (Albuquerque: University of New Mexico Press, 1991).

12. Richard Rodriguez, *Days of Obligation: An Argument with My Mexican Father* (New York: Penguin Books, 1992), xviii.

13. Rosario Morales, "Puerto Rico Journal," in Aurora Levins Morales and Rosario Morales, *Getting Home Alive* (Ithaca, N.Y.: Firebrand Books, 1986), 76, 79.

14. See essays in Behar, *Bridges to Cuba*, especially Maria de los Angeles Torres, "Beyond the Rupture: Reconciling with Our Enemies, Reconciling with Ourselves"; Flavio Risech, "Political and Cultural Cross-Dressing: Negotiating a Second Generation Cuban-American Identity"; Ester Rebeca Shapiro Rok, "Finding What Had Been Lost in Plain View"; and Rosa Lowinger, "Repairing Things."

15. Cristina Garcia, *Dreaming in Cuban* (New York: Alfred A. Knopf, 1992).

6. Anthropology That Breaks Your Heart

1. Thich Nhat Hanh, *Present Moment Wonderful Moment* (Berkeley, Calif.: Parallax Press, 1990), 73.

2. Américo Paredes, "On Ethnographic Work Among Minority Groups," in Ricardo Romo and Raymund Paredes, eds., *New Directions in Chicano Scholarship*, Chicano Studies Monograph Series (San Diego: University of California, 1979); Angie Chabram, "Chicana/o Studies as Oppositional Ethnography," *Cultural Studies*, special issue on "Chicana/o Cultural Representations: Reframing Alternative Critical Discourses," 4 (1990): 242; Renato Rosaldo, "Chicano Studies, 1970–1984," *Annual Review of Anthropology* 14 (1985): 405–427; José Limón, "Representation, Ethnicity, and the Precursory Ethnography: Notes of a Native Anthropologist," in Richard G. Fox, ed., *Recapturing Anthropology: Working in the Present* (Santa Fe, N.M.: School of American Research Press, 1991).

3. See, among others, Gloria Anzaldúa, *Borderlands / La Frontera: The New Mestiza* (San Francisco: Aunt Lute Books, 1987); Cherríe Moraga, *Loving in the War Years* (Boston: South End Press, 1983); Sandra Cisneros, *Woman Hollering Creek and Other Stories* (New York: Random House, 1991); Alicia Gaspar de Alba, María Herrera-Sobek, and Demetria Martínez, *Three Times a Woman: Chicana Poetry* (Tempe, Ariz.: Bilingual Review Press, 1989).

4. Roy G. d'Andrade, "What *Do* You Think You're Doing?," *Anthropology Newsletter* 36, 37 (October 1995): 1, 4.

5. Not all anthropologists are sorry to lose the culture concept. Many have long preferred to focus on "political economy," while others now focus on the concept of "class." For a valuable critique of

the limitations of the culture concept, see Lila Abu-Lughod, "Writing Against Culture," in Fox, *Recapturing Anthropology*. Yet even if the culture concept is discarded or replaced by other concepts, we must still contend with the issue of what makes anthropology distinctive as a discipline.

6. Paul R. Gross and Norman Levitt, *Higher Superstition: The Academic Left and Its Quarrels with Science* (Baltimore, Md.: Johns Hopkins University Press, 1994), 256. Also see Evelyn Fox Keller, "Science and Its Critics," *Academe* (September–October 1995): 11.

7. David B. Givens and Diane Manheney, "1994 Survey of Departments" (Washington, D.C.: American Anthropological Association, 1994), 288–299.

8. Michael S. Roth, *The Ironist's Cage: Memory, Trauma, and the Construction of History* (New York: Columbia University Press, 1995), 226. My warmest thanks to Deborah A. Gordon for bringing Roth's work to my attention.

9. Renato Rosaldo, *Culture and Truth: The Remaking of Social Analysis* (Boston: Beacon Press, 1989), 1–21, 168–195.

10. Claude Lévi-Strauss, *Tristes Tropiques: An Anthropological Study of Primitive Societies in Brazil* (New York: Atheneum, 1967), 388.

11. Homi K. Bhabha, "Dance This Diss Around: On Victim Art," *Artforum* (April 1995), 19–20. Also see Bill T. Jones, with Peggy Gillespie, *Last Night on Earth* (New York: Pantheon Books, 1995).

12. Roth, *The Ironist's Cage*, 225–226.

13. Roth, *The Ironist's Cage*, 225.

INDEX

Abu-Lughod, Lila, 205n5
African diaspora, 148–49
Afro-Caribbean identity, 148
Agee, James, 5
Agoraphobia, 124
Alienation, 24, 51, 63, 130
Allende, Isabel, 1–2
Allison, Dorothy, 162
Anthropology, 4–5, 25–26, 82, 172; and bones, 174; Chicano critique of, 163, 175; of death, 21, 84, 86; and humanists, 166; identity crises of, 163–64; "native," 27–28, 166; as science, 6, 165
Antonio Maceo Brigade, 140
Anxiety, 6, 9, 10, 42, 102, 163, 176; of influence, 171
Anxiety attacks, 30, 119–126
Anzaldúa, Gloria, 22, 27, 175
Argentina, 84
Ariès, Philippe, 45, 49, 55
Autobiography, 12–13, 18, 175; African-American, 27; of childhood, 132–34; commercialized, 25; feminist approaches, 28, 30. *See also* Personal narrative
Aztlán, 149–50

Benjamin, Walter, 42
Bhabha, Homi, 176
Bloom, Harold, 171
Boyarin, Daniel and Jonathan, 147
Bread, symbolism of, 56–59, 62, 68, 198–200nn19–20
Brecht, Bertolt, 154
Bridges to Cuba (Behar), 154–55
Buñuel, Luis, 40

Casa del Poeta, 154
Castro, Fidel, 111, 140–41, 145, 152–53, 154
Cemetery, 52, 65–68, 70, 89–90
Chicana writers, 163, 175
Chicano movement, 150
Childhood, 127, 142–43
Christ, 47, 54, 56, 199n20
Christianity, 54
Cisneros, Sandra, 132–34, 175
Class, and ethnicity, 133
Clifford, James, 200n32
Coe, Richard, 132
Community, 32, 56, 59, 62, 198–200nn19–20; of memory, 78–79
Compassion fatigue, 86
Consumerism, 62–63, 79–80

Croce, Arlene, 175–76
Cuba, 18, 22, 23–24, 32,
    71–72, 111, 117–18,
    137–161; arts in, 138–141;
    criticism of, 153; dreams
    of, 152, 154; as forbidden
    territory, 149
Cuban Americans, 22, 92,
    97–98, 111–113, 121–22;
    ambivalence toward Cuba,
    151; difficulties of visiting
    Cuba for, 137, 141, 144,
    145, 156; of the second
    generation, 140–41, 142,
    149, 151, 154–55, 157;
    status in United States,
    117–18, 150
Cuban culture, 144–45; race-
    less image of, 118
Cuban diaspora, 145–46, 148
Culture concept, 164, 204–5n5
Culture of terror, 84–85

Davis, Natalie Zemon, 199n25
Death: as defeat, 85; denial of,
    66; fear of, 79; in hospi-
    tal, 49, 51, 53, 55; Jewish
    customs of, 69–70, 75–76;
    as journey, 47; in rural
    Spain, 43–68; "tame," 49;
    traditional, 53–55
De Beauvoir, Simone, 30–31
De Certeau, Michel, 34,
    81–82, 85–86
Delibes, Miguel, 39
Depression, 9–11; and women,
    30–31, 132
Detachment, 17–18, 25, 64
Devereaux, George, 1, 5–6, 7,
    8, 16, 28

Diaspora, 21, 143, 145–149,
    150
Dubisch, Jill, 83
Duty-memory, 42, 61, 68, 81

Elkin, Judith, 84
Emigrants, 135
Emotion, 167, 171–72, 174,
    175; and academic settings,
    17–19, 21–22, 178; and
    death, 54, 76; and intellect,
    boundary between, 86
Empathy, 21–22, 127
Estévez, Rolando, 157–58
Ethnicity, and class, 133
Ethnographic authority, 21,
    172
Ethnography, 6–7, 20, 175,
    200n32
Evans-Pritchard, E. E., 7
Exile, 145

Fabian, Johannes, 84
Feminism, 28–30, 171, 174, 175
Fernandez, James, 197–98n9
Fieldnotes, 8–9
Fieldwork, 8, 34, 173
Folklore, 44, 47
Fowler Calzada, Victor, 155,
    159–161
Franco regime in Spain, 38

Gates, Henry Louis, Jr.,
    128–29
Geertz, Clifford, 5, 7–9, 28
Geographies of time and
    space, 140
Gilligan, Carol, 131–32
Gilroy, Paul, 148
Ginsberg, Allen, 160–61